Law
and
Disorder

J. J. Casale

ISBN- 978-0-578-87540-8

"AFTER ENOUGH TIME HAS PASSED, ALL MEMORIES ARE BEAUTIFUL."

~ AUGUST STRINDBERG

PROLOGUE

The stories are all true. Only the names and places have been changed to protect the guilty. In the years I served with the "thin blue line", many stories were stored away in my memory awaiting opportunity to be revealed. Such a time has finally arrived.

The pathos, bravado, tears, comedy, and sheer humanity of those with whom I served, demand their story be written. The experience of writing has given my life a new dimension. I hope it does the same for the reader.

Those who served:

Chief Wildman

Deputy Director "Jay" Castle

Detective Chin

Detective Hendershot

Lt. Halinger

Sgt. Salterella

Sgt. Hendley

Ptlm. Millstone

Ptlm. Cameron

Ptlm. LoSanta

Ptlm. Elders

Ptlm. Prohaska

Ptlm. DeQuinto

Ptlm. Wallerstein

CHAPTER 1

THE ALIENS HAVE LANDED

It was one of those stifling hot July nights, the kind that makes your pores work overtime. The incessant drone of the straining air conditioner was punctuated by the staccato reports on the police radio.

My name is Jay Castle. I am the Deputy Director with the Southbrook, Illinois Police Department. I was working my usual desk watch of the graveyard shift, 8 p.m. to 4 a.m. My one patrol car was working with the one and a half mile of our little "purgatory" known as "The Boro". It was a rare occurrence to have both our patrol cars in operational condition at the same time. Our small community of 5,000 souls had tight budget restrictions, and the Police Department was on the low end of the priority scale. Underpaid and overworked sounds trite, but it was the way of life in our town.

The three-room Police Station's desk was dimly lit by a fluorescent fixture, flickering on the edge of extinction. I was attempting to catch up on the days paperwork on a typewriter that must have served as a prototype for the first-ever Remington, when the ringing of the phone aroused me from my frustration. I glanced up at the clock to mark the time of the call. It was 2 a.m. The male voice on the line was edged in hysteria.

"Hello, Police? A large flying disc just landed in my backyard and they….they are trying to get into my house!"

"Who are *they*, sir?" I replied.

"Who *are they*? How the hell do I know, God dammit. They just got out of that thing that landed!" was the reply.

1

"Sir, can you please briefly describe these beings?" I continued.

"Hell, yes. They are looking through my window right now!" the caller replied. "They are about 3 feet tall with flat heads and red glowing eyes."

I took down his name and address, assuring him I would dispatch a car immediately. In retrospect, I would have promised to dispatch the United States Marines to get him off the phone! By a sudden spark of inspiration, I glanced out of the window. There was a full moon. "Of course", I thought to myself. "Weirdo time" has snuck up on me again. (The weirdos come out of the woodwork during a full moon). I keyed the microphone on the police radio to call my patrol car. As luck would have it, I had the perfect officer to respond to the call. Our number one "weird" cop, Philo Elders. I pushed the "transmit" button on the radio. The rest became legend.

"Base station 699 to car 28", I intoned.

"Car 28, by", replied Elders.

"I have a report of a flying object that has landed behind the residence of 18 Franklin Street. Talk to the male resident. He reports small creatures with flat heads and glowing red eyes attempting to gain entrance into his home."

A long pause on the other end. I chuckled to myself in anticipation of Philo's befuddlement.

"26 that message, 299?" requested Elders. He requested a repeat of the information.

After my initial call to Philo, all the stations on our frequency went strangely silent. They were listening to our chatter. Heck, it was a slow weekday night. This was the most interesting event this week if you don't counter the Puska Farm pigs getting loose on Highway 206, being sent to "bacon" heaven by heavy traffic!

My mind briefly wandered to the famous 1938 "War of the Worlds" radio broadcast. I'll bet it started the same way. Only tonight we were "flying with Philo".

"Car 28 to 699. I'm 12 this location." (He had arrived at the scene). It was a few minutes before I heard from Car 28 again. Normal procedure would have been to call for the patrol officer to make a preliminary written report and then inform the base station that he was clear from the scene. But this call was not normal, and neither was the responding officer! Philo proceeded to make his report over the airwaves.

"699, the creatures were GOA (gone on arrival). The subject reported these gnome-like creatures attempted entry via his back door and window, but they were frightened away by his screams and the arrival of my vehicle." ("Like most of the neighborhood") I thought to myself.

"Car 28 will be checking the local cemetery. It's a favorite *haunt* for UFOs in the area". Philo's puns were as bad as his police work.

Suddenly, as if a floodgate had opened, a cacophony of calls jammed the airways at the station. The nearby towns, including the Park Police, asked if they could help us in our "saucer hunt". The voices were less than sympathetic. You could hear raucous laughter in the background. County Police called to report that one of their cars had sighted our "saucer" and had given chase. "Car 28 to 699. I'm on a '30' with evidence of the saucer." (The car was coming into headquarters).

The screech of brakes at the back door of headquarters signaled the arrival of Philo the "saucer hunter." As his large stomach breached the doorway, his loud laugh responded to my ever-widening grin.

"What evidence do you have, shithead?" I inquired.

"This!" Elders held a bottle of clear liquid at arm's length. "It's the saucer's fuel supply", he continued.

I inspected the bottle that was thrust upon me. It had contained 150 proof vodka. "It sure fueled this nut's imagination", I thought out loud.

Now my problem was how to write up the events in the police blotter. I decided a straight-forward account was in order. I was going to tell it as it happened. It was going to make for some interesting reading in the morning paper. In red pen, I marked the entry line. Subject: "Flying Saucer Lands, Aliens Attack Home." The Chief's day would be made when he read the entry. He would be off on one of his early morning rages and make life miserable for everyone that day.

"Hell", I thought. "Crime is nasty business. Even if it is perpetrated by beings from another planet." Besides, this episode was shooting straight to the top of my list of strangest proceedings ever witnessed. But as would be later revealed, it wasn't even close.

CHAPTER 2

THE WARNING

The Police Department of Southbrook was located on the first floor of a dilapidated building. Over the entrance was a sign that read: Municipal Building. I remember with great clarity my first day on the job at police headquarters. That was ten years ago. I was being briefed on my administrative duties by Sergeant Vincent Salterella. The sergeant was a soft-spoken, intelligent officer, but in the late stages of "burn out". You've seen the kind before, the type that rookies crowd around asking for advice. Vince had seen it all. It showed in his face, the tired eyes, the lines in the furrowed brow.

His talk was interrupted in mid-sentence by an exasperated voice. "Sarge, I have to talk to you…right away…in private." The last two words were underscored in his voice. It was Sgt. Hendley.

Hendley was an imposing figure of a man, standing 6' 4", weighing every bit of 200 lbs. He had a scowl that could make a corpse twitch. Hendley gave a cursory glance in my direction and continued speaking. "Can you get rid of the civilian? (I was in street clothes). Besides, it's a rule not to have civilians behind the police desk."

Sgt. Salterella took the criticism from the junior sergeant in stride, looking up with those weary eyes and speaking out. "Sergeant Hendley, I'd like to introduce you to our new administrator, Jay Castle."

Hendley fell silent, looked again in my direction and I saw the look in his eyes. It was one of impatience. He briskly extended his hand in my direction. "Glad to meetcha", he blurted out. He then swept Salterella aside to speak in hushed tones away from earshot.

I had a gut feeling we were not going to get along. In retrospect, it just goes to show you how wrong first impressions can be.

Hendley, having finished his conversation, again approached me. He seemed a little less tense now, and grinned as he spoke. "So, you are our new administrator?" he began.

"Yeah", I replied. "I'll be working the desk on the 8 p.m. shift."

"Man, you are in for it. Just wait till you are working here alone at night. You'll wish you had taken up some other line of work. Rarely a dull moment late at night in this town.

Now, I was raised in one of the toughest parts of a nearby city. I stand 6 feet tall and weigh 186. I hold two belts in two different types of karate. I am a survivor and have the scars to prove it. I was an expert rifle and pistol shot. What could possibly happen in this tiny town that I could not handle?

I was about to find out.

CHAPTER 3

SODOMY AND GOMMORAH

The doldrums of the first week ended abruptly on Wednesday morning at 3 a.m., to be exact. I was working on a mundane traffic report, when the front door of the Municipal Building swung open with such force, the walls rattled. Before I could react, the hallway door was also thrown open.

My initial reaction of surprise turned to fear, as a screaming man raced through the doorway toward the railing that fronted the police desk. He hit the railing so hard the momentum hurled him across the desk. Oh, and he was naked!

Sgt. Hendley's words resounded in my head as I reached for my service revolver. "Just wait til you are alone at night". Damn! My weapon was frozen in its holster. I tugged at it again, all the while keeping both eyes on the intruder. It was later that I discovered I had neglected to first release the strap that bound the weapon to the holster.

The man was lying outstretched over the desk, his face a twisted distortion. Saliva rimmed the corners of his mouth, intermingling with his cascading tears. Failing to free my Smith and Wesson .38, I pushed back hard from the desk. I jumped up as the chair fell over. My only thought...."get to the microphone and summon aid."

Suddenly, he reached out his hands in supplication. For the first time, I looked into his eyes as the desk illuminated his face. His screams had subsided into heaving sobs. The eyes and gestures were pleasing for something his voice failed to yield. They were asking for help.

"Can you talk?" I yelled. My heart was pounding so loudly that yelling seemed to be the only way he could be heard.

"Yes", he hissed softly. "The dirty sons-a-bitches…the no good bastards…they…they"…his voice trailed off. "They did what to you?" I persisted. "They….they raped me…." His voice broke into sobs.

Further attempts to get more information was pointless, except I was able to get the location of the assault. It occurred under the bridge that connected our towns of Southbrook and Eastbrook, after some late-night drinking on our side of the bridge.

"I'll get some help", I reassured him as I keyed the mike to transmit. I was also reassuring myself.

"Bas 699 to Car 27 or 28…'30' to headquarters. We have a WHISKEY MIKE (white male) at base that appears to have been sodomized", I remember saying.

I looked down at his pathetic shattered form, stripped of human dignity, as tears of rage and compassion welled up in me. I shut off the desk, lamp and slowly walked to the back to await the patrol car and the officer in charge. The episode has lasted only a few minutes, but in my mind, it would last an eternity.

The "man" was 18 years old.

Now, a sex crime is a barbaric crime. Never in my life would I have thought of it in any kind of humorous light. Except once. That night, during my second week on the desk, Sgt Hendley was pulling patrol duty.

The woman was completely nude as she strolled into headquarters. Her ample breasts pressed up against the brass rail that fronted the desk. She had my attention.

"Hey, officer, I've just been raped", she stated rather matter-of-factly. I was embarrassed and surprised by her calmness. Taking off my jacket, I came around the desk and draped it across her shoulders. I ushered her into a chair and tried to get a description of the perpetrator.

"The attack happened at Marwhich's Rooming House," she said. The assailants were described to me as two male Hispanics, approximately 18 to 20 years of age, both with slight moustaches. She also described their clothing.

I called for the patrol car and then phoned for a detective, as both detectives were off duty. Within moments, Sgt. Hendley arrived. I furnished him a description of the suspects and directed him to the scene to pick up a few articles of clothing for the woman. Detective Hendershot arrived about 10 minutes later, his eyes still blurry from sleep. It was 4 a.m.

After a few preliminary questions, she was brought a few pieces of clothing and sent to the Rape Crisis Center of Somerdale Hospital for examination.

Hendershot attempted to piece together the story. He asked me if I noticed anything unusual about the victim. I replied that she appeared to be very calm for such an experience, but that she most likely was in shock.

"Also", said Hendershot, "there was no evidence of trauma. No bruises or signs of any physical violence." He looked at me with a wry smile.

"Ah, come on Detective (my favorite name for Hendershot), there may have been a weapon involved", to which he responded, 'no', there was no weapon involved according to the victim's statement.

Detective Hendershot was sharp. Young and energetic, he was very good at his job. Six feet tall, dark curly hair, handsome features and a wide, straight-toothed smile. He was a woman's dream come true. He had sensed something was not right in this case. His senses did not often fail him.

Hendley's voice broke over the radio. "Car 27 to 699, have two suspects that fit your description, in front of the cemetery on upper Main Street. Request backup." Hendershot bolted out the door and pushed the patrol car to the limit as it careened out of the driveway, lights and siren blazing.

Our detective was given to over-exuberance at times, but I chalked it up to youth. The suspects were brought into headquarters and I set eyes on them for the first time. Two, very scared Hispanic youths were ushered in wearing handcuffs. They shook like wet puppies. Hendershot read them their Miranda rights, and waiving their right to an attorney, the questioning began:

Hendershot: "We have a woman who states you guys attacked her at Marwhich's Rooming House. You both admit to being there with her. What is your version of the story?"

Suspect #1 (Carlos) – "No man, she ain't been raped. No way, Jose, this dude ain't done nothin' wrong. She did it for $20. That 'puta' wanted more, but I only had a 20.

Hendershot: "You mean she asked for money to perform a sexual act?"

Carlos: "Yeah, wanna $50 but I have just $20. So she take it."

Suspect #2 (Juan) – "Si, officer. It happen like that. Like my compadre say. We met her at bar, have a few drinks….my buddy ask if she would come back to his place. She wanted $50. Carlos, my buddy, he jus have $20, so she say she do it for $20, hokay?"

Hendershot: "Ok, Carlos agreed to $20. Now, did you get into the act?" addressing Juan.

Juan: "Si, I mean, yes."

Carlos: "We walked back one block to my pad. We go in, have a few more drinks. She take off her clothes and we start, you know, doing it."

Hendershot: "And where is Juan now?"

J. J. Casale

Carlos: "Oh, yea, he watch man…you know we only have $20."

Hendershot: "If he is watching, how come the lady says you both raped her?"

Silence followed…. there was a long pause and both suspects looked at each other. Tears welled up in their eyes.

Carlos: "It was my buddy, Juan, that got us messed up!"

Juan: "Hey man, I can't help it. I got so hot watching you, I just had to do something!"

Hendershot: "What did you do, Juan?"

Juan: "Dios Mio! I just was watching him there; I try to get in on the action somehow."

Hendershot: "By doing what?"

Juan: "Well, by sticking it in her…"

Hendershot: "Let me see if I have this right. You mean while your buddy, Carlos, was having sex with her, you attempted anal sex? Is that correct?"

Juan: "What you mean, man, anal?"

Hendershot: "Her ass."

Juan: "Si, si, is what happen…" Then she yell like hell, jump up and ran out!

Further investigation corroborated the stories. The sequence of events as told by the two boys was verified by the 'victim'. She had prior convictions for prostitution. Carlos was released on minor charges. Juan was indicted and found guilty of sodomy and attempted fellatio. Juan got seven years. Even whores got rights.

CHAPTER 4

CAR 27: WHERE ARE YOU?

I love a mystery. At least I did, until the night of October 20, 1976. Standard operating procedure mandates that the desk officer call the patrol car for radio and location checks every half hour, if no other contact has been eliminated in the interim. The procedure allows the desk officer to know the unit's location and serves to keep the patrol officer "on his toes."

On this chilly October night, the wind was ripping at the old municipal building like the claws of a hungry tiger. The cold seeped through the cracks in the window, creating an eerie sound as in a gothic horror movie. Salterella and I were working at headquarters, trying to rearrange the schedule. There were many sick calls during the past week. Patrolman Cameron was working the only available unit, car 27.

About 2 a.m., Salterella started to feel the effects of a virus that had decimated our ranks. First, he began to sweat profusely, then he complained of nausea and stomach pain. I told him to go home and rest for a while and check in if he felt he could not complete his shift, to call for a replacement. After all, he lived only a few blocks from headquarters and I had Cameron in a patrol car, so I thought.

At 3 a.m., the bars let out their usual stream of human refuse. Since it was midweek, the activity level should have been non-existent as far as police calls go. I had yet to commit to memory the axiom, "expect the unexpected!".

Neighboring Eastbrook crackled to life with our call sign. "Eastbrook to Southbrook '699', we have an altercation in progress at the Low-Life Tavern. Request your car to back our patrol at the scene."

Eastbrook had three times our manpower and about the same edge in patrol cars. So, when they called us for backup, it was a good bet that it was a full-scale war.

The familiar sense of adrenalin surged through me, as I hit the key to summon my car.

"Base 699 to Car 27, you copy Eastbrook's call?" My voice quivered in anticipation.

Dead silence. I repeated the call and again, silence. After a few minutes, the urgency level rose to anger, "Dammit, Cameron", I swore, "Answer!" My calls went unheeded.

"Eastbrook to 699, where the hell is our backup? We have a 'pier 5' over here!"

I could hear screams and cursing in the background of the Eastbrook call. Perspiration broke out on my brow, and I could feel the dampness under my arms trickle down my sides. My calls, which by now had turned into impassioned pleas were as yet unanswered. Ten minutes had passed.

"699 to Eastbrook, I am unable to comply with your request for backup. I am unable to raise the patrol car. Please request additional support from another locale."

My voice trembled with humiliation and frustration. The unwritten code of reciprocation had been violated, the code every cop lives by, and sometimes dies by. You back up an officer when requested, or someday when you need backup, they will reciprocate in kind.

Running the gamut of emotions, fear now raised its ugly head. For Cameron. Perhaps he had been a victim of some unknown assailant or had a cardiac arrest and was lying there helpless. I call Salterella on the phone.

"Jesus, Vince! I can't raise Car 27. I have been calling for him for 12 minutes and I get no response. I proceeded to outline the course of the previous events. Still sick, Cameron came back to headquarters and started out in the unit to search for Cameron. Vince allayed my fears and assigned the problem to radio failure. I wasn't too sure. One hour had passed. Cameron surely would have been aware his radio was not functioning by now and would have come in.

Utilizing cars from other nearby communities, Eastbroook cleared up its brawl and radio went silent.... except for an occasional forlorn plea to Cameron.

The feeling of letting down a fellow officer and the possibility of someone being hurt as a result left a bitter taste in my mouth. I did not know at the time it would not be the only incident of its kind to happen in our division. Two hours passed. Still no sign of Cameron. Damn!

After the third hour, I was about to close headquarters and go out of my own to search, letting Franklinville to handle our dispatches. I also toyed with the idea of calling the Chief, which I quickly dismissed. Chief Wildman (or "wild man" as he was called behind his back), was too irrational to handle it at this hour. Also, I should get the story and find out what exactly happened out there.

Suddenly.... success! Salterella's voice sounded like he had won the lottery. "699, I've located Cameron. He's okay. We'll be on a '30' to headquarters." Finally, after 3 and ½ hours of suspense, Cameron walked into the back door of the station. LaMonte Cranston Cameron, alias "the Shadow", stood there red-eyed.

"What the fuck happened to you?", I exploded.

Salterella quickly interjected that it was not Cameron's fault. He had been ill with the flu the last couple of days. Too little sleep and some medication he had taken before going out on patrol made him drowsy and he had fallen asleep. He was sleeping behind the local gas station on Main Street.

"You fell asleep?" I asked incredulously.

15

Yep, Cameron had slept like a baby through the entire episode. Slept, while I was agonizing at headquarters.

I slammed my first down on the desk, shattering the glass cover into a maze of slivers. I turned and looked at them both and walked out the back door. It was hours past my relief, and I had had enough!

The cold wind felt good on my perspired face. Suddenly, I was exhausted. Cameron's small portable radio in the patrol car caught my ear as I passed the open window of the marked unit. A familiar song was playing: "Life is just a bowl of cherries, don't take it serious, life's too mysterious…" I shook my head and went home.

"Where's my backup?" were the last words the Franklinville policeman yelled into his radio. It was January 1977. The new year had been rung in for two weeks. Lieutenant Halinger was working the afternoon desk watch that cold, sunny day. A Franklinville patrol car was in hot pursuit of a vehicle entering our Boro. "Car 401, 699" the car called our base. "Am in pursuit of a green Vega on Raceway Avenue. Request backup."

Car 401 was occupied by Officer Bart Emory, a hulking, gruff, no-nonsense policeman. Halinger was annoyed by the call. He was immersed in paperwork, and the call distracted him from the task at hand. He was a fine administrator. His round cherubic face belied a strong sense of conviction. Desk duty was right. Chasing around in patrol cars was wrong. Halinger made no move to the radio.

Unfortunately for Emory, the road car for Southbrook was tied up at the County Jail in Somerdale, delivering a prisoner. Halinger was the only officer in our Boro available to respond to the backup call. Halinger's face twitched in indecision.

"Franklinville to 699. Have vehicle stopped on Raceway Ave. Your Boro. Request support." Emory snapped over the radio.

Halinger fidgeted about his desk, straightened his tie, tugged at his cuffs and made a decision. He got up from his chair, walked back toward the rear. Once there, Halinger pounced on the remaining jelly doughnut left on the table, returned to the radio and lowered the volume. The annoying chatter belabored his ears. Now the noise was barely audible.

"No problem", Halinger thought to himself. As he picked up where he left off, he thought he heard the Franklinville officer saying, "Where's back...."

As big as he was, 6' 6", Emory had his hands full after his last transmission. The three occupants of the Vega, spaced out on some narcotic, did not take kindly to Emory's attitude. So much so, they attempted to separate the officer's head from his shoulders with a tire iron! The sergeant's nightstick and large fist separated two of his assailants from their senses. The third, in the meantime, road Emory's back like a mechanical bull.

Another Franklinville patrol car, hearing Emory's repeated calls, arrived on the scene about the same time as an Eastbrook patrol car from across the river. The four officers quickly restored tranquility to our Boro.

With the prisoners safely put away in the cars, Emory had one more stop to make, Southbrook Police Headquarters. The code of reciprocation had been broken, and he was determined to find out why.

As his large frame pushed through the back door of our headquarters, his swollen right eye alighted on the feverishly writing Halinger at his desk. Emory was aware of Halinger's reputed reluctance to provide backup. Emory felt the flush of heat up his spine as he strode the remaining few feet that separated the two men. As he did, the sergeant heard the muffled voices over the police bank. Suddenly, the questions in his mind were answered. Halinger swing around in the swivel chair and caught the look in Emory's eyes. The

17

Southbrook police officer's eyes widened in fear as the front of his shirt was gathered into a tight ball by Emory's fist.

"Now I know why you didn't back me up when I called and called and called!" Emory's voice was tight and deadly calm. The sergeant's free hand reached over and raised the volume of the base radio.

"You son-of-a-bitch!" Emory's voice spat out. "If I EVER call for backup when you're on duty, you WILL respond, or I'll come and get you. Then I'm going to scatter your brains all over that desk!"

Emory spun around and calmly walked out the back door. He didn't bother to turn the screen door handle, he just walked through it.

Halinger had not uttered a single word. He just stood there twitching as if in the throes of St. Vitus' dance.

Charges and counter charges flew over the incident, but it was conveniently buried, as are many inter-departmental squabbles, lest the public catch wind of them. One very interesting fact did emerge from the incident…it seems the Southbrook PD has, to this day, no written police procedure or conduct. Every officer sort of learns through experience. On-the-job training, taken to its ultimate refinement.

Oh, and yes, Emory retired in 1980. Between the January 1977 incident and the retirement in 1980, Halinger managed to change shifts or call in sick every time Emory drew patrol in the area nearest our Bobo. NO PROBLEM!

CHAPTER 5

PAC MAN

Swapping Halinger stories became a religious ritual around headquarters. Whenever a couple of officers got together, especially when Rookies were present, the tales began. It was reminiscent of a telling ghost stories around the campfire.

Halinger's reputation for non-intervention in matters outside headquarters was exceeded only by his fabled appetite. On an evening in March 1977, I was working, on my birthday. I had brought in six cupcakes left over from a party thrown for me earlier. I entered the station via the back door and placed the white powdered confections on a small table in the dark room.

Sitting down at the desk in the adjoining room, I assumed my nightly duties. Around midnight, Halinger lumbered in through the rear door for his midnight to 8 a.m. shift. I heard him unlock the Chief's office from the adjacent room and switch on the lights. No words were exchanged.

After a few hours, I put on a fresh pot of coffee and went to the back room to retrieve my goods, my mouth watering in anticipation of the delicacy. I picked up the bag, immediately puzzled by its lightness. I was angry. The bag was empty!

"Hey, Halinger, did you touch the bag on the back table?" I called out.

Halinger stepped out of the Chief's office. He replied he had seen nothing. His voice was muffled. I switched on the lights. Mystery solved. The corners of Halinger's mouth as well as his tie and shirt, were covered with tell-tale traces of the powdery residue. I had made my first encounter with the Boro's answer to "Cookie Monster".

19

To the uninitiated, the number 30 is insignificant. To Halinger, it was a language fixture. In police parlay, '30' meant return to headquarters. He would '30' his road patrols into paranoia. Even during eating breaks and bathroom breaks, that '30' would seek out the errant officer and bring him to the station, at Halinger's every whim. As a result, when he rode the desk, the patrols found themselves judiciously guarding the citizenry from the rear steps of headquarters. The officers we had, hated the situation. They knew their job was to be out on patrol and not chained to the rear of headquarters. Unfortunately, by virtue of his rank, the men came whenever they were '30'd'.

A minor conspiracy developed among some of the patrolmen. Their measure of revenge would be to hit him where he was most vulnerable, his stomach. Every time Halinger took his eating breaks, the road officer would come in to fill in at the desk, squad calls and firecalls dictating this measure.

The officers struck with a vengeance. Halinger would no sooner clear the driveway than he would get a '30'. Halinger, his stomach growling, would be sent on some inane escort or call. The retribution went on until Halinger complained to the Chief. Separating Halinger from a meal was like separating a hungry lion from its kill. The order was posted over the police desk. "No routine calls are to be assigned to the Lieutenant while he is on break. Such calls will wait until he has completed his meal."

The course of action gave way to one grand act of deprivation that came to me in a blinding flash of constipation! It is fondly remembered as the "Lemon Pie Caper".

Halinger's favorite delicacy for his evening forages were the Taystee Lemon Pies which he would consume in bulk. Woe to the officer who failed in his quest to ferret out these morsels when summoned to do so.

One such evening, a new officer, Patrolman DeQuinto, was dispatched on such an errand of mercy. A local convenience was open 24 hours and had on hand the last remaining supply of lemon pies. While on his way to the store, DeQuinto spotted a driver leaving the parking lot at high speed. The driver further neglected to stop at a Stop sign in his hurried departure. With lights flashing and siren blaring, DeQuinto pursued and stopped the culprit a few blocks from the store; whereupon, the officer stepped out of his vehicle and proceeded to administer justice.

No sooner had he taken out his summons book when a call came over #3 channel, reserved for emergency air traffic.

"699 to Car 27 on 3", Halinger radioed. "27 on 3", DeQuinto responded. "Where are my lemon pies", Halinger said. "Uh, I'm on a motor vehicle stop and will be issuing at this location", DeQuinto responded. "I want those lemon pies NOW; do you hear me?" demanded Halinger.

Halinger was agitated, but before DeQuinto could respond further, the lieutenant ordered him to 'cut loose' the driver and respond back to headquarters with his '31' (food pickup). DeQuinto was understandably 'pissed' but he had his orders.

The patrolman stuck his head through the window of the waiting motorist and spoke through clenched teeth, "Sir, I am going to let you off with a warning. I have an emergency to get to. An officer at headquarters is near death with 'shrew's disease'.

"Shrew's disease?" the motorist queried. "I don't believe I've heard of it."

"Yes, it's a rare malady. The officer must eat his weight every day or die of starvation!"

DeQuinto walked away from the puzzled motorist and turned the patrol car toward the store. Lights and siren all the way down the street.

When I heard the story the next day, I somehow had to strike a blow for justice. Revanche! (revenge) prompted the scheme that I nurtured in my imagination.

The next evening there was a light mist of rain on the Boro. It was one of my 'off' days and the same two officers were working together. I put on an old trench coat that was at least 20 years out of style. It had been shoved in the back of the closet and somehow never given to the Salvation Army. I pulled up the collar and sent to the late-night store. Casually, I strolled up to the clerk, cigarette dangling from my lips. He was alone.

"Hey, kid", I said. "How many Taystee Lemon Pies you got in the joint?" in my best Humphrey Bogart impersonation. He pointed, "Just those over there", he was shaking. Either my Bogie was great, or he thought he was about to be the victim of a robbery.

"Great, give me a paper bag. I want them all!" The corners of my mouth even twitched as I spoke. I walked to the display and swept up the pies, 25 in all. There would be no lemon pies to be had in our Boro for a while.

"You sure like your lemon pies, don't you?" inquired the clerk as he totaled up the sale on the register. "Ten bucks mister", he said. "Say it again, Sam", I lisped. "I said, you sure like your lemon pies, and my name isn't Sam…. it's Rick!" "Figures" said I.

As I walked through the door, I spoke over my shoulder. "If anyone asks what happened to all the lemon pies…. tell 'em, Victor Lazlo bought them all." I walked out into the rain. I could have sworn I heard the faint drone of an airplane engine as I got into my car.

For the following few weeks, whenever Halinger came in on his different shifts, he found an empty box of Taystee Lemon Pies in his mailbox. Sometimes a note was attached to the box. A little 'taunt' from "Lazlo". Too bad Halinger had probably never seen Casablanca. He would have enjoyed it. Too bad he didn't notice the 6 lbs. I had gained recently!

HERE'S LOOKING AT YOU, HALINGER!

CHAPTER 6

THE FENWICK 'CUCKOOS'

The Fenwick Apartments had several inhabitants with 'partial decks'. Our town had more than its share of fuzzy thinkers and the police always wound up dealing with them at one time or another.

The night was unusually warm for June. It was 1977. I was working my usual post at the desk. The old expression, "When it rains, it pours", was about to take on new meaning for me. The evening was moving at a snail's pace. Even the normally active police radio begain "snoring" with a hushed zzzzzzz.

The feces hit the windmill with a resounding thud at 2 a.m. The shock wave caused me to fall over in the swivel chair. I jumped to the window in time to catch a bright orange ball rising up from the old manufacturing plant. My first impression was that we had been "nuked" in a surprise Russian attack. I then saw the flames shooting skyward and black acrid smoke billowing from the site. It was big!

I hit the general fire alarm that set the town sirens off, and dispatched one of my cars to the scene. It was one of those rare nights that I had both "clunkers" on the road. I hit the rescue squad plectron radio to alert them to respond. My job was not to sit back and log the calls and handle radio traffic. With the Boro sirens still blaring, the phone rang.

"Police? Send the squad to 17 Warren St., a man is having a heart attack." I hoped it wasn't the sirens that brought on the condition. I keyed the microphone. "699 to Car 28, proceed to 17 Warren St. Heart attack in progress." I hit the plectron a second time to inform the squads of a second call for their services. Now I had all the fire apparatus with horns and lights outside my window. Two police cars with lights and sirens, going to different locations. The Boro sirens wailing and two ambulances and a light truck going God knows where! The end was not in sight. The phone rang again.

The caller informed me that there had been an auto accident at the corner of Edgemere and Cedar Streets. I was in shock.

"699 to any car. When you are clear....M/V accident at Edgemere and Cedar Streets. No injuries....Thank God."

In the space of 10 minutes, I was exhausted. One cannot imagine what the police radio sounded like while sharing our radio frequency. At this time, for some depraved reason, "Marie the Mouth", a nearby police station dispatcher, decided to get the shotgun numbers from all twelve of her patrol cars. She never got past her second car.

The phone at headquarters rang again. I was almost afraid to answer. "Hello, Officer? My name is Louise", the caller began. "I live at Fenwick Apartments, 16-B. My son said I have a beautiful body. I am only 36. Would you like to come over and look at it yourself?"

I could not believe what I was hearing. Every conceivable form of Boro siren going like hell, police, squad and fire bands stepping all over each other, trying to get their messages out, and now, some broad inviting me to a Comparative Anatomy class! Even my deodorant was failing me at this point! I explained what was going on in town and that I would have to call her back. I hung up, thinking to myself, "If a police dispatcher dies...and goes to Hell...this is what the punishment must be like." The phone rang again. "Hello, officer? It's me again, Louise. Officer, I'm so lonely. There's no one here to look at my beautiful firm breasts." "Lady, look", I said, "I'll send someone over in just a few minutes, okay?" I said resolutely. I slammed down the receiver.

26

"Car 28-699, squad has arrived and is transporting victim from Warren St. to 5-0 (hospital). What's your pleasure?"

Well, my pleasure was at 16B Fenwick Apartments, but I was stuck at headquarters!

"Car 28. Go to Apt. 16B (as in Baker) Fenwick Apartments. See the lady. She has a libido problem.

"699 repeat. You were cut out. A what problem? Liver problem?"

"Never mind, Car 28. Just go." I said wearily.

Sgt. Salterella knocked on door 16B. He was also very tired. The door opened wide. She stood there, in the open doorway, without a stitch of clothing. Vince's eyes widened. He thought he had died and the gates of Heaven were just opened.

"Hi. My name is Louise. Please do come in. I have a beautiful body..."

The sergeant closed the door behind him. He was like a moth drawn to a flame. He managed to convince her to dress and it wasn't more than five minutes before I heard him arriving at the station. Things were beginning to quiet down, and I drew from the desk a blank report form. The top of the form had the usual physical description of the subject; age, color of eyes, hair, etc. When I began questioning Salterella, he did not reply. Then with a sheepish grin, he spoke: "You know, Jay. I never once got a look at her face!"

We both laughed until tears fell. We later learned that Louise, along with a group of others, were just out of a regional mental clinic. The clinic had established a halfway house at Fenwick Apts. They called it "mainstreaming", an attempt to gradually expose their patients to the outside world under the supervision of a Counsellor. Somehow the police department was not informed of this situation. The names of the patients

27

in residence and their counsellor was finally made known to us.

I never did get to meet Louise. Maybe it was for the best. I can't help but wonder....would I have been able to describe her face?"

◊ ◊ ◊ ◊

In addition to the strange occupants of the Fenwick Funny Farm, the town had several other colorful characters. We referred to them as the "Community Crazies." All had crossed our paths at one time or another. To wit:

SCREWDRIVER MAN: The nemesis of Sgt. Hendley, so named because he carried the aforementioned tool in his belt. Hendley once had the rather dubious honor of taking him to Veterans Hospital in the back of his squad car. It was to be a voluntary commitment. The trip there was frightening, as the man leered at me from his straitjacket, smiling his all-knowing smile. Halfway back to the station, we received a call to go back and pick him up. Seems he wasn't a veteran! The squad refused to go back for him. (Rescue squads abhor transporting mental patients). The mere mention of "Screwdriver Man" coming into headquarters would send Hendley fleeing in a patrol car. Oh, did I neglect to mention, he was also Hendley's next door neighbor?

SHEETMAN: "Sheetman" walked around the Boro dressed only in a sheet and sandals, claiming to be a messenger of the Messiah. He never really bothered anyone; that is, until he hacked his mother to death in a nearby town. He drove to the State Capitol and threw her severed head onto the steps of the building. He also received twenty write-in votes in the last mayoral election.

JUNGLE JOE: Alcoholic, ex-councilman, he was forced to resign from office when convicted of flashing two teenage girls. He became a penniless "bag person", attempting to get criminal records expunged. He slept in a cardboard box at the back of local taverns. He was later appointed "Special Police Officer."

THE AXEMAN: Alias, "Spanish Joe", twice nearly killed Sgt. Hendley with his favorite device, a double-headed axe. Some of the officers say that the two encounters with the axe is what gave Hendley his "split" personality.

BIRDMAN: Ex-local cop, he kept getting himself arrested for impersonating a police officer. He had his vehicle equipped with dashboard mounted flashing red light and concealed siren. He patrolled Boro's lover's lane. To him, Caryl Chessman was a folk hero! He was finally convinced, along with a local postal inspector, of molesting a young girl.

THE HERMIT: Dwelt in a dilapidated mansion until his untimely death at 96. He constantly called headquarters due to prowlers (that later proved to be imaginary). It was said he had a large fortune hidden somewhere in his home. He received special attention from Lt. Halinger because of Halinger's interest in the hermit's well-being. Upon his passing, Halinger was bequeathed a million dollars…in Imperialist Russian Czarist War Bonds.

ATTILA THE HUN: The owner of the "Animal House" bar. He suffered from delusions of grandeur and paranoia. He sometimes walked around town with the actual hat worn by Napoleon Bonaparte. Emblazoned on the hat was the French expression "L'Etat C'est Moi", (the state is me). After failure in business, he voluntarily exiled himself to Helena, Montana.

THE CELLAR DWELLERS: Numerous local denizens who inhabited the "never-never" land of the bridge and tunnel that connected the towns of Eastbrook and Southbrook. All mental deficients whose acts of vandalism, rape, sodomy, drunkenness and necrophilia, littered the police logs of both

Boros. The only law left unbroken was cannibalism, as far as we know.

CHIEF WILDMAN: He was a definite certifiable case, as you are soon to discover…

CHAPTER 7

THE HARWICH HORROR

Patrolman Millstone was every inch a cop, all 5' 6" of him. He may have been small in stature, but there was no other cop I would want to have my back in a tough situation. He was tough, and smart. A thick black moustache added to his menacing countenance. His nickname was "Shoes" because he like foot patrol so much. And, always the half-smoked cigar in his mouth. (His teeth did not clench the cigars because he carried them in his back pocket!) The original set of teeth were long gone, falling prey to his numerous run-ins with scumbags. The guys on the force were waiting for the day when, in some fashion, his dentures would have a life of their own and finally bite him in the ass. One more thing about Millstone, when you worked with him, things were never dull. He seemed to draw our local psychotics out of the woodwork.

It all started as a routine call. They all do. The call came late Saturday, just before midnight. The young woman caller had heard someone pounding on her door at the Harwich Rooming House. These one-room apartments were a favorite gathering place for indigents, looking for a place to flop for five bucks a night. The caller requested a police officer. She suspected the pounding was her next door neighbor, whom she told me was "very strange". Harwich was one block from headquarters.

As usual, I had just one patrol car, Unit 27. Car 28 reposed behind headquarters with terminal transmission issues. Millstone was in Car 27. He was just about to be relieved of duty, and his relief, Wallerstein, was coming in the back door of the station. "Shoes" volunteered to check on the call. Routine call. "Some drunk unable to find his room, creating a disturbance", Millstone thought as he eased his unit to a stop at Harwich.

31

Knocking on the door, the officer identified himself and was let into the dimly-lit room. The officer proceeded to the back of the apartment near the kitchenette. Millstone started his report for the log., paying little attention to the sealed off door that adjoined the caller's apartment.

The fist exploded through the upper wood panel of the door with such suddenness and force that Millstone was unable to avoid the crushing blow. The reflex action of moving his head back from the noise, saved him from taking the full impact upon his head.   The huge, hairy hand grazed Millstone's temple, knocking him off balance.   Millstone rebounded off the floor in time to see a foot smashing through the bottom panel of the door. Millstone reached for his mace with one hand and his walkie talkie with the other. He braced for the impending onslaught of his shadowy antagonist.

"Unit 1, Code 1, gimme backup fast!" Millstone barked into the radio. Wallerstein and I both heard the Code One priority. It meant, "Officer under attack, send everything". I spun around in the chair as Wallerstein was "hitting" the back door. "Never mind the God damned car! Foot it over to Harwich's", I yelled after him. As luck would have it, it was just a one block run. And, luck really had an important role in this, with only one patrol car. In retrospect, I wondered what would have happened if this incident had taken place further from the station.

"The Hulk" had by this time smashed his way into the caller's apartment and was face to face with Millstone. The officer raised his mace can and sprayed him right in the face. It didn't even seem to faze him as he bore down on Millstone. Two more desperate squirts from the can also had no effect. "The Hulk" reached out his hand and seized Millstone by the throat, shaking him like a limp puppy. Millstone dropped his radio and withdrew his lead sap from his hip pocket. Small gurgling sounds came from Millstone's throat as his truncheon cracked his assailant on the side of his head. "Hulk" fell, stunned, into a crumpled heap.

Wallerstein, guided by the woman's screams, flung open the apartment door, gasping for breath. Wallerstein slid behind the assailant and brought his nightstick down on the crazed attacker. Blood from a gaping head wound covered the man's face.

The arresting officers brought their quarry to headquarters, where he was patched up, awaiting the arrival of the First Aid Squad. He stood 6' 2" and weighed over 200 lbs. He just sat there snarling and grunting like some primeval cave dweller. I was nervous just being in the same room. We went through his wallet to get information for an arrest card. I counted 10, $100 dollar bills in there.

"What is that Trogdolyte doing with all this money in a five-dollar-a-day flop house?", I questioned the officers. Neither of them had an answer to my question. But we got our answer the following Monday. A search warrant for his room revealed a quantity of drugs. He was a "Candy Man", an itinerant drug dealer in town on a deal. We called the County Jail, where the man was being held, in order to detain the prisoner pending new charges. We received bad news. "The Hulk" had made bail and was released. He was never seen again.

"Shoes" was none the worse for wear. He did get a day off to see a doctor on Monday. It seems he had to have a doctor look at what appeared to be human tooth marks on his left buttock!

CHAPTER 8

A LIFE WORTH SAVING

"God told me to do it!" the wimp of a man squeaked. He spoke for the first time, as he sat handcuffed to the chair at headquarters. Weighting about 115 and about 5' 2" tall, it was hard for me to realize that it had taken three officers to get him where he now sat. His head shaven and bowed, a mixture of blood and water dripped from his brow, onto the grimy floor. Mr. Hall, sitting there with his torn T-shirt with the word "REPENT", looked like a poster child for CARE.

The three of us, Millstone, Salterella and I, sat around him, unable to fathom what compulsion drove him to attempt to murder his one year-Old child!

I had requested to ride patrol that evening, as Salterella had some paperwork to complete. He would handle the desk, and I would ride with Millstone. The change of pace would do me good, I thought. I need to log some patrol time to keep me current. My education was about to take a Quantum leap.

We were working radar on Main Street, when the call came that jolted our collective nerve systems.

"699, Unit 27. Fenwick Apartments, 4A. Man attempting to kill his infant." Salterella's crisp call hung in the air like a stench.

We hit the lights and siren. The patrol car groaned into action as Millstone punched the accelerator.

"Unit 27, 699" Request backup at said location", Millstone left nothing to chance.

The car careened to a halt at Building 4. Both of us were out of the unit before it had time to come to a complete halt. Both of us were out of the car. Seconds counted. My heart was overdosing on adrenalin, as I made the stairs to the first landing without touching a step. Guided by the screams of Mrs. Hall, Millstone and I reached the door. "Shoes" glanced at me and I nodded. We flattened ourselves against the wall on either side of the door, hands on weapons. I reached for the knob. It was locked. Both of us took three steps back. I counted to three. We both kicked with all the strength we could muster. The blow splintered the jamb and the door swung open.

The scene that met my eyes is one I've reserved for special nightmares. You know, the kind in which you wake up screaming, bathed in sweat. The open bathroom was directly in sight. A kneeling man was holding a struggling form submerged in a tub full of water, while his half-crazed wife was pawing at his back and shrieking.

We had crossed the room before the sound of the splintering door had died in the dusk. Millstone grabbed the man by his hair and yanked him backward. I seized his hands, attempting to release his grip on the child. Neither of us was successful. The little boy was as strong as an Italian cigar. Millstone and I abandoned our course of action, just as Salterella flew into the room. All three of us commenced to beat the sucker onto the floor. The patrolman maced, sergeant hit him with his lead sap and I ricocheted my nightstick off his testicles. He moaned and pitched forward into the tub. Two of us went along for the ride. The sergeant grabbed the still-struggling baby.

Luckily, his wife had fended him off just prior to our arrival. The kid was going to be okay. As I walked out of the building through the throng of curiosity seekers, I made a vow to myself. In the future, if I wanted riding time, I would avoid Millstone's shift and ride with Halinger. I knew then I would be able to steer clear of trouble….NO PROBLEM!

CHAPTER 9

THE CHIEF WHO COULDN'T SHOOT STRAIGHT

Chief Wildman measured up physically to what my image of a Chief of Police should be. Crewcut greying hair, clear ice-blue eyes and rugged handsome features. His uniform was always immaculate, and his motto was "Everything must be neat and clean, clean and neat!" This included the ashtrays in the patrol cars.

Not so long ago, the Chief found ashes in the ashtrays of the units. It offended his senses and he removed the ashtrays from the cars. The patrol officers began using the next most convenient solution for the problem, using the floors for the ashes. Someone neglected to inform Patrolman Prohaska of the ashtray removal. Prohaska smoked cigars. While driving, he would stick his fat cigar into the "hole" where the ashtray would have been. The acrid smell of burning plastic alerted him that something was amiss. A huge misshapen hole in the center of the dashboard gaped out at the Chief on the morning's car inspection. For days afterward, Wildman sat in his office brooding like some modern-day Othello. Every day for a week a new special order appeared on the desk of the incoming day watch, and I quote:

Day 1: No smoking in the patrol cars.

Day 2: Officers-in-charge will inspect cars at the end of each shift to ensure #1 is carried out.

Day 3: Cars will be swept and cleaned after every shift.

Day 4: Any officer caught smoking in a patrol car will be suspended.

Day 5: No butts or ashes in cigarette trays at headquarters.

Day 6: No smoking at headquarters.

Day 7: Officers will be searched for contraband cigarettes before leaving in a patrol car.

This went on, AD NAUSEUM, and as a matter of course, everyone ignored the daily postings.

The Chief's wrath finally settled on our resident chain smoker, Patrolman Millstone. Millstone dreaded working the day watch with the Chief. Everyone did. It was like doing penance for past sins. The patrolman was the antithesis of the chief, untidy, easy going and chain-smoking. Everything Wildman hated!

A typical conversation between the Chief and Millstone started out in the following manner:

"Millstone, what the Hell are you doing? Sleeping in uniform? What's that on your tie, ashes? Have you been smoking in the patrol car? Millstone, you are a mess! I'm going to suspend you. Sergeant Salterella, put Millstone on report! Ugh, you guys…. you think I'm kidding? Hey…."

The Chief had a way with words, one syllable, four-letter words, that is. They sprinkled his vocabulary like raisins in a bowl of raisin bran. They poured forth profusely, non-stop. He was the only man I ever knew who could use "fuck" five times in a ten-word sentence!

Ah, but this was his better side. For fifteen years he ruled the department with all the demeanor of Camp Commandant of Auschwitz, playing one officer against another to satisfy his own inadequacies, until everybody on the force was paranoid. A game of Russian Roulette, with human psyches for bullets. Expose a vulnerability to Wildman and he would exploit it until he broke you. That was…until he met his match in yours truly!

The Chief was more than a little intimidated by my educational background. I had completed my undergrad work and was beginning my Masters, and he couldn't "psyche me out" as easily as the others. The Chief had always maintained a posture that refused all requests for reimbursement or rescheduling for officers taking Police Science Courses to further their education. Nor were there any provisions for salary increments to those officers. He discouraged any educational advancement of officers. To put it mildly, our relationship was tenuous. Sgt. Salterella and I were among the few who could speak to him when he closeted himself in his office during his frequent rages.

My very first meeting with Chief Wildman sort of set the tone for our relationship. Needing arm patches for my new uniforms, I intruded on the Chief in his office. At first, I had tried to get the patches from Hendley and Salterella. Both men said they were very difficult to obtain and that I would have to see the Chief. I was in luck the day I entered his office. Nothing had gone wrong and he seemed to be in a good mood.

"Caswell, Caswell, come in!" he said. Wildman also had a penchant for mispronouncing names. I explained that I needed patches. He very quickly opened a cabinet, snatched some patches and closed it again. Despite the speed at which he did this, I couldn't help but notice the huge supply on hand. One whole shelf of tightly banded arm patches. The shelf was 4 feet long and a foot high. There appeared to be enough patches to supply all the needs of the Chicago Police force. I was surprised to find this amount, as we had only a 14-man department.

When he noticed my queried expression, his mood grew dark. He gruffly explained that "some previous Chief" had spoken to a salesman about ordering a small number of patches, about 30. While engaged in conversation with the salesman, the long-gone chief signed a contract for the patches, which, by the way, had to be specially made. The chief; however, forgot to check the number ordered. When the Boro Council got the invoice, the howls could be heard across the river in Eastbrook. The order amount contracted, on which a deposit was made, read 300 patches. "Goddamn slimy snake-oil salesman really screwed the Chief", Wildman exclaimed smugly.

When I recounted the story to Hendley and Salterella, in an attempt to ferret out that long-gone Chief's name, they both smiled broadly. I did notice something else later on. Chief Wildman always delegated the signing of all contracts on his behalf to Sgt. Salterella!

One of the responsibilities I had as Deputy Director was coordinating the annual weapons qualifications for the regular, special and auxiliary police. When Millstone, the range officer, submitted the names of those to fire weapons on the following Saturday, one name was conspicuously absent, the name of Chief Wildman. When I suggested that Millstone ask the Chief to qualify, he looked at me with the same expression he had when he dropped his false teeth in a pile of manure. "What? You crazy? Me? No way!" he exclaimed as he walked out the door. As the Chief was an officer and carried a weapon, I felt he should be qualified with its use. The Police Commissioner agreed when I spoke with him on the subject.

The following day, both the Commissioner and I stepped into the busy station to speak to the Chief. Suddenly the normal activities of the station ceased, as each officer found an excuse to leave. I smiled to myself. They sensed a tremor about to happen, something akin to animals lying down in a field before an earthquake. It was general knowledge that Wildman hadn't qualified with his sidearm in 15 years, or since he had become Chief.

The Commissioner spoke first. He tactfully suggested that it would be good for the Chief to show up at the firing line on qualification day. "Leadership showing the way", was how he put it. The Chief would have no part of it. "Me?

Qualify?....hey, besides, ugh...I've got an appointment with my proctologist", the Chief lied.

"Well, I've got just the cure for your ass, Wildman!" the Commissioner replied. He handed the Chief a written order and a list of shooters with Wildman's name at the top. The Chief was subdued. He took the subtle hint. "I'll need a .38 caliber with a long barrel. I don't want to use this "snub nose" .38." He withdrew his personal sidearm from its holster to show us the small 2" barrel.

Both the Commissioner and I saw the same thing at once. The bullets in the chamber of the revolver were covered with corrosion. Before the Chief could re-holster his sidearm, the Commissioner stayed his hand and took a closer look at the weapon. The barrels inside were spotted with patches of rust and verdigras.

As the Commissioner walked out of the office with me in tow, he whispered to me, "That damn weapon hasn't been fired in years!", to which I added sardonically, "Those bullets must have been original issues, which would make them about 20 years old".

Saturday came. Qualification Day broke bright and sunny. Everyone showed; regulars, specials and auxiliaries, including two seldom-seen faces, Sgts. Hendley and Salterella. I should have said "everyone showed except Chief Wildman." Millstone, the range officer, told me the Chief had called in sick and would qualify the next day, Sunday, at 10 a.m. (I made a mental note to be at headquarters tomorrow to ensure that everything went as scheduled).

Sunday morning, I rushed to the Police Station at 9:45 a.m. to catch the long-awaited moment. As I was about to enter headquarters, I was met by Millstone in a patrol car. "The Chief ready to qualify?" I asked. "He already has", replied Millstone. He held up a tattered target for me to see.

The range officer avoided my eyes as he shuffled past me into the office. I took the target from him and held it up to the light. Many of the holes were uniform and perfectly formed. They showed no evidence of edge-tattering that the wade cutter bullets usually show. They were also a shade smaller, about the same size as the #2 pencil Millstone used to mark the targets.

The range incident faded into obscurity when compared to the magnitude of Wildman's next blunder.

Chief Phillips of the Franklinville Police was visiting Chief Wildman during one of his infrequent visits. The discussion turned to the safety merits of the shotguns that our patrol cars carried. Ours carried a type of shotgun or "Riot" gun that had two build-in safety features. Essentially, they had two buttons, one that must be pressed to load a shell into the chamber, and another that must be depressed in order to fire the weapon.

Our Chief wished to make some vague point to the visitor. Millstone was working the road in Car 28, and Sgt. Hendley was on desk duty on that fateful day. Wildman asked Hendley to ask Millstone to "30" to headquarters with his car shotgun. Here's where the plot thickens.

Millstone, unknown to the Chief, had just gotten back into his car after responding to a bank alarm. The alarm proved to be an accidental activation. Not knowing the alarm was false, Millstone had chambered a shotgun round upon arrival at the scene. Upon ascertaining everything was in order, Millstone responded to Sgt. Hendley's "30" signal, intending to unload the gun at headquarters.

The argument between the two Chiefs was pretty heated by the time Hendley walked past the Chief's office to open the back door for Millstone. In walked the benign "Shoes", carrying the loaded "riot" gun. Wildman heard the voice of the patrolman and scurried out of his office. Our Chief assumed Millstone had pulled the normally unloaded gun from the car rack. "Christ, it's about time you showed up!" Wildman exclaimed, as he yanked the gun out of Millstone's hands. The officer hadn't the faintest idea what the boss was talking about. Our leader whirled around, about to say something to Chief Phillips. He never got to complete the sentence.

The deafening roar of the discharged shotgun shook the entire Municipal Building. Various employees ran into headquarters to see what had happened. Our Chief stood speechless for the first time since the doctor had slapped his rump upon his birth.

The curious onlookers beheld a scene right out of "Gilbert and Sulllivan". Hendley stood leaning against a backroom locker. Two inches from his head was a large fresh dent in the steel locker door. Opposite the Sergeant was a gaping hole in Chief's room wall. A large wet stain was permeating Hendley's pants in the area of his crotch. Millstone was bowed over holding both ears. The Chief stood quivering, the smoking shotgun in hand. Chief Phillips stood in the doorway of the office, his mouth agape, his lips trying to form words that defied verbalization.

No formal report of the incident exists. It has been handed down from mouth to mouth from who experienced the incident, with all the reverence of the Gospels before some scribes translated them into the written Word. Millstone lost partial hearing in one ear, a loss that indentured him to the department for the rest of his career. He would never have been able to pass the physical of another police force should he have chosen to leave. Chief Phillips never set foot again in our headquarters. In the fifteen years that intervened until his retirement, Phillips never mentioned Chief Wildman by name again. His occasional reference to that "gold-braided asshole" was understood. Everyone knew who he meant.

One incident involving Chief Wildman is a matter of record. It was recorded on the tapes of the County Police. The County routinely tapes the messages that are transmitted across the radio band we share. It was heard over the airwaves by those who cared to listen. Too bad many of the listeners did not recognize the voice they heard.

One busy afternoon I was working a rare day shift. I was attempting to piece together a state grant for some new Mobile Radar Units. It was 1977 and our police cars did not have mounted radar units. The one model of radar they did have, a hand-held unit, was forced down the Chief's throat last year at my instigation. Attempting to bring our department out of the "stone age" of communications was a never-ending battle between the Chief and I. He had the temerity to remove the teletype machine from the department because he thought it of no use to our police work.

The Chief graced my desk with his presence. Did I say "graced"? Hell, he plopped right on top of it, Wildman was in rare form. One could tell, because when he felt good, he spoke on his favorite "macho" subject, the female anatomy.

The Chief was rather explicit in his choice; namely, the upper anatomical structure of the gender, the breasts. Wildman arranged himself atop my desk, back toward the radio, facing my seated form. The police microphone for the base radio was also on the desk. As a matter of fact, the Chief sat on top of the microphone base. The transmit button is, coincidentally, built into the base of the microphone. So, when the Chief sat partially atop the base, the transmit base depressed and our leader's monologue became recorded history. I heard the faint "click" as the red transmit light flashed on the console. His back to the console, he did not realize he was "on the air".

"Hey, Caswell", the boss addressed me, "You like bit tits on a woman?" I suppressed a fleeting desire to tell the Chief what was happening. It was only a momentary twinge of conscience. "To tell you the truth, Chief, I really don't give it much thought, working here", I responded. "Well, I have." Wildman indulged in his "stream of consciousness". "I love 'em! Does your wife have big tits?" "Monstrous", I replied. "They're so big she has to have a special bra designed by the same designer who created the structural supports for the B-52 Bomber." The Chief was impressed. I could tell by the look of envy on his face. "I never met your wife, have I? Why don't you bring her down to headquarters and let me get a look at her?" the Chief said. He was trying to be as nonchalant as possible. "God Damn! Just how big are her boobs?" The Chief pursued his fragile train of thought. The train was about to be derailed.

Wildman's voice grew so agitated that he did not hear the voice on the police radio calling out, "Whoever is making those comments over the air, your radio is keyed open. Knock it off!"

I mentioned the "Wildman's" name every opportunity I got. Despite this, there were at least a full three minutes of lewd commentary by our town's ranking police official. When the phone did ring, I knew the "shit had hit the fan". It was Chief Garibaldi of the Eastbrook Police. "Wildman! You screwball, your voice is being heard all over the County. Your damn transmitter is keyed on!" Garibaldi yelled over the phone. The Chief tried to disclaim it was his voice. "Hey, me? It isn't me!" Then, as he denied in vain, he looked down where he was sitting. The light was finally penetrating the darkened recesses of his prehistoric brain. He suddenly sprang from the desk. He looked incredulously as the red transmit light clicked off the console. The Chief stared for another few moments at the microphone and quietly swore under his breath. He handed me the phone and gruffly told me to switch the call to his private office phone. The dragon disappeared into his lair, a spear through its heart.

From time to time, I heard his raised voice swearing vehemently behind the closed door. I smiled broadly. My day was made. I was glad also that this was my only day shift. I would sure hate to be working day shift during the rest of the week, or month, depending upon whether the County Prosecutor's Office had overheard the episode.

CHAPTER 10

ELEGY

The days of Summer, 1977, were dwindling. I had come in early to attend to some piled up paperwork. Sometimes I think paper has a life of its own, that, after all the lights are out, late at night, the paper breeds in triplicate.

The omnipresent phone rang. On the other end was a distraught female caller. She reported her child missing. I requested the physical description of the missing child and the clothes he was last seen wearing. I broke my pencil underlining the last item on the preliminary report, his age.... three years old!

The patrol officers arrived at the house within moments of my dispatch. The backyard in which the young boy was last seen was enclosed by a chain link fence. The fence gate was secured from the outside. Preliminary thinking was that the child had scaled the fence ad was in a neighbor's house or yard.

An expanding circle-type search was initiated. It is a type of pattern that starts from the point of last contact, and fans out in an ever-widening circle. Time passed with no positive results. An hour before dusk, more volunteers were requested, and I went in with some volunteer rescue squad workers. The detectives questioning the single parent determined that she had left the child in the backyard while she went to her neighbor's house for coffee, a time span of about two hours.

It had now been four hours since anyone had seen the boy. A Franklinville Police officer spoke to me in passing. He too was an off-duty searcher. "Can you beat that? She's sitting for two hours, bullshitting at a neighbor's house, and doesn't one check to see if her kid's alright!" he spoke disgustedly.

The yard from which the youngster had vanished contained an above ground pool. The securely covered pool stood four feet above ground, with no deck or ladder to climb. It was given a quick look under the cover. Nothing.

Darkness was settling in. More volunteers were requested to help. Search teams scoured the surrounding area with no results. The detectives on the scene were beginning to lean toward a kidnapping and prepared a County-wide alert. Everyone concerned with the search had an uneasy feeling about how the events were unfolding. The neighbors hadn't noticed any strange cars around the area. Many had been outside in their yards and would have noticed the child or any stranger. The town was small. Everybody knew everybody. As stranger would have stood out like Sammy Davis, Jr. at a KKK rally.

Night fell and trucks from the rescue squads utilized their floodlights to aid in the search. The stabbing beams of illumination added an eerie component to the hunt. I made a hasty departure for a few minutes to pick additional flashlights and batteries. Sadly, the search was over.

I heard a voice, flat and unemotional, over the radio, "The boy has been found." I wheeled my car around and hastened back to the scene. I discovered why the voice lacked emotion.

As I arrived, I saw the focus of the floodlights to be the backyard pool. My heart stopped. An officer was emerging from the water with the limp form cradled in his arms. I pushed through the frozen pack of spectators. The child's sightless eyes shall forever live in my memory. They starred but saw nothing. Some volunteers sobbed softly, as if their tears could somehow change the horror they beheld. The mother's anguished wail pierced the still night air. An officer feebly attempted CPR on the form, but the spark of life was long since gone. "Breathe, dammit, please…. breathe!" another worker muttered imploringly. I don't cry often. Only two other times as an adult. Once, when my father died and once when my son, Ethan, died. I cried now, openly and unashamedly. Many old wounds in my memory were opened that night. They blew anew in the rush of forgotten memories. The ones we all try to forget but never really succeed.

A Franklinville Police Officer was the first to discover the body. He and another searcher had, on some unknown impulse, decided to take the cover completely off the pool. Their probing flashlights made the grisly discovery. The body was lying on the bottom of the opposite end of the pool that had been quickly eyed during the first search of the area. No one knows how that tot scaled the 4-foot side without aid. No one ever will.

The stillness was broken by a crackling ambulance radio, "Rescue Squad, 18E, we're Code 2 to hospital…from the scene." The officer's voice cracked as he spoke.

I walked slowly from the scene, leaving that place of senseless loss. To this day, whenever I pass that home, I remember that evening. I always will. As I departed, I thought of the Epitaph I had inscribed on Ethan's gravestone, some lines from a cherished poem:

DO NOT STAND AT MY GRAVE AND WEEP

I AM NOT THERE; I DO NOT SLEEP.

I AM THE SUNLIGHT ON RIPENED GRAIN

I AM THE AUTUMN'S GENTLE RAIN…

I AM THE SWIFT RUSH OF BIRDS IN FLIGHT

I AM THE STARS THAT SHINE AT NIGHT.

DO NOT STAND AT MY GRAVE AND CRY,

I AM NOT THERE; I DID NOT DIE.

CHAPTER 11

HENDLEY'S NEW HAIR

The Dog Days of August 1977 had taken their last bite. Fall had crept in, and the leaves put on their Autumnal display of color. Falling leaves carpeted the ground like Nature's rug. Sgt. Hendley also acquired a "rug" this Fall. A new hairpiece! Worried about his receding hairline, which was receding faster than the value of the US dollar, Hendley took the bold step to bolster his "macho" image.

Everyone at headquarters noticed the first time he wore it on the job. You couldn't help noticing it. He must have gotten it at a bargain sale at "Crazy Eddies". No one said a word. Hendley had come into headquarters expecting the usual barrage of irreverent humor, but not a word was spoken. The suspense began eating at him. He waited for the proverbial "other shoe to drop". He didn't have long to wait.

The word had gotten around about his recent acquisition, so everyone was prepared for the grand entrance. Patrolman Cameron, however, could not contain himself. He possessed a small cassette tape recorder which he kept in his locker. As Hendley went about the day's routine, Cameron loaded the recorder with a tape he had bought that morning. He put the cassette atop his locker and turned the volume as high as it would go. Cameron pushed the "play" button and exited quickly out the back door. A rendition of a popular movie and Broadway play blasted throughout the stationhouse. The theme song from "Hair" reverberated. As his fellow officers shrieked with laughter, Hendley tore through the station to find the source of this blatant attack on his new image. "God damned idiots! You got no respect for a senior officer?" he extolled as he ferreted out the recorder and removed the offensive tape. My stomach hurt from laughing.

Hendley's problem with his toupee had just began. The glue used to set the piece into place lost its holding power when the perspiration wet his scalp beneath the uncomfortably hot "Trooper" styled hat.

One sunny Autumn afternoon, Hendley pursued and caught two young women zipping down Main Street. His radar clocked them at 45 mph in a 30-mph zone. Dutifully, the officer put on his overhead red lights and pulled over the "young foxes". Hendley put on his official scowl as he approached the driver's side of the car. "License and registration please". His police introduction was flawless in its execution. The two young ladies were attired in the briefest of shorts. They glanced at each other and giggled. Hendley started to sweat more profusely as the driver leaned over to retrieve the papers from the glove compartment. Her loosened blouse revealed, to the delight of the officer, she wore no bra. Hendley's face lost its official scowl, replaced by a small grin.

After checking the documents, the sergeant handed the papers back to the driver. "I'm letting you off with a warning. Please be more careful how you drive. You were in excess of 15 mph over the speed limit." Hendley lifted the brim of his hat in a parting gesture of gallantry, and that's when tragedy struck.

As the girl started the car, a black hairy "creature" plopped between her well-tanned bare thighs. She screamed as the car lurched forward and struck the curb. Hendley's hairpiece had become unglued and, when he raised his hat, it fell from his head. Now it was Hendley's turn to become unglued. He approached the screaming pair and retrieved his errant interloper as it was ejected from the auto. He was further mortified, when the girls, realizing what it was, began laughing uncontrollably.

The sergeant began to attempt to apologize, realized it was for naught, and ran back to the patrol car.

As he was about to enter the back door of the station, Hendley flung the disheveled prosthesis disgustedly into the air where it landed on the low hanging roof of the back door. Eventually, a pair of birds took up housekeeping in its warm confines. The crestfallen sergeant never wore a hairpiece again,

SIC GLORIA TRANSIT.

Hendley was a talented man. He could sing, dance and was an artist and impersonator. His reputation with the women was also way above average. In fact, his prowess with the ladies was only exceeded by his prowess with the bottle. The latter may have been the fatal character flaw that bound him forever to this department and its misanthropic Chief. I always marveled at his characterizations when we worked together. I had a saying about Hendley; i.e., "When he frowns, dig a hole in the ground. When he smiles, everything is reconciled." His impersonation of Richard Burton singing "Camelot" was genius, as were his impersonations of Chief and Halinger. Visiting policemen would convulse during his imitations.

One evening Hendley and I were riding patrol. Hendley was in a grand mood. He was taking requests for songs. There wasn't a title I could think of, but that he knew the words and lyric. "Have you ever thought of singing professionally?" I asked. "Naw" was his reply. "I don't have the balls to do this in front of a real audience." "Pity", I said.

I picked up the car microphone to call in our location. The sergeant began crooning a lovely ballad which he knew was one of my favorites, "Feelings". As I sat next to him, mesmerized by the rich quality of his voice, a warped thought slithered its way into my mind. It was 3 a.m. on a slow weekend. Even the radio was sleeping…. I had the microphone in hand…it was about time that Hendley made his debut on the air, I thought. "What the hell, I can always plead insanity." (In our department, I would likely get away with it). I keyed the microphone open and laid it to rest between us.

As he concluded his rendition, clapping and yelling could be heard on the frequency. Someone who apparently recognized Hendley's voice, broke in with "Atta boy, Hendley!" The police car nearly swerved off the road as the befuddled sergeant realized that he had been broadcasting. "How…. what…how could they…." He stammered. Hendley quickly looked at me and then down at the seat between us. He saw the microphone in my hand. "Jesus Christ!" he swore. "You had that mike open the entire time?" The look on my face made the question superfluous. The cheering over the radio continued, "Encore, encore, one mo' time!"

I grinned sheepishly. "I just had to let the folks out there in radio land hear that voice", I said. Hendley was beside himself with apprehension. The front seat of the patrol car was getting crowded. I brought the microphone to my mouth in in my best announcer's voice intoned, "Live, from our remote pickup, the lilting rendition of "Feelings" was brought to you by…"

Hendley jerked the mike from my hands and replaced it on its hook. "Man, you crazy!" he yelled at me. The three-minute ride back to headquarters was dead silence. As he shut off the motor, he made no move to get out. He sat there for a minute, then turned slowly to me and spoke, "Was it really that good?" I laughed out loud. I replied it was but that if he wished further confirmation, we could take a quick ride up to the "County Mounties" and get the transcript of the monitored police band. "Don't bother", he stated emphatically, "they've got a lousy ear for music."

CHAPTER 12

PISS ON PALKO

"Southbrook Rescue Squad, you have a Code 12, with fatalities…River Road, Franklinville". I was in my own vehicle when the call came over. Since I was near the location, I drifted toward the scene to give assistance.

The month of January 1978 had its share of many accidents in and around the Boro, but nothing more gruesome as the scene I was about to witness. The driver of the wrecked vehicle was being pursued by an Eastbrook patrol car driven by Patrolman Frank Carino. He had chased the vehicle through our town and had called Franklinville to head off the speeding driver at River Road. As the speeding vehicle rounded an icy curve, he lost control and plunged down the steep embankment to the water's edge. The guard rail had impaled the driver. He was dead before the car stopped rolling.

I saw the driver's head hanging out of the window of the vehicle as I peered over the embankment. A Franklinville officer was already on the scene, coming up from the car as I arrived. He had ascertained the driver was the sole occupant. "Anything I can do, Herb?" I asked the officer. "Naw, the dude's gone", he replied. He should know a dead person when he saw one. Officer Herb Weiner had seen his share of corpses in Vietnam, many of which he had personally "wasted". He had also been cited for bravery twice as a police officer. He had slain three bank robbers singlehandedly about two years prior.

Weiner and I went way back. I had taught him in school years ago. Then, he was a happy outgoing kid of fourteen. He didn't smile much now. Killing sometimes can have that effect on a person. Somewhere between Vietnam and that shootout two years ago, Herb forgot how to smile.

Frank Carino had finished his written report and joined the group standing on the shoulder of the embankment. He had been busy with the radio and had also put up flares for oncoming traffic.

Weiner turned to Carino. "Do you know who you were chasing?" Carino shook his head no.

Herb looked into Frank's eyes…" you should, it's Palko". Carino broke into a wide grin. "Palko! That dirty scumbag. You sure?" Frank started down the incline toward the wreck. He called back to us. "This I gotta see for myself."

"Who's Palko?" I asked Herb. "Palko is the dirt bag that raped Carino's sister a couple years back. He got out on parole after serving only 10 months. It's one of the reasons Frank Carino became a cop. He swore someday he would get Palko. Guess fate beat him to it." It looked like Carino's hunt was over. We turned and watched Carino near the overturned vehicle.

By now, Carino was satisfied that it indeed was Palko. He looked up at us and I heard him yell,

"He sure looks good dead!" Carino straddled the corpse's head, unzipped his fly and began urinating on the deceased. "Are you seeing what I'm seeing?" I asked in an incredulous tone. "Yep", replied Herb. "Some feelings transcend even death."

The squad was now approaching the scene. I motioned to Herb. "Get Carino the hell out of there fast! I'll stall the squad a moment." It wouldn't be easy explaining an officer pissing on a corpse's head, especially to the female membership.

Weiner retrieved Carino from the wrecked car and I left the scene. I saw the two officers shivering in the blustery cold through my rearview mirror. It was the last time I ever saw them.

A month after the death of Palko, Frank Carino resigned from the police force. He had come from a well-to-do family and I could never understand why he had become a cop, until I heard of Palko. He left the state and last I heard he was living in Florida. I guess being a copy had lost its "Raison d'etre".

Herb Weiner went too. After his marriage broke up, he blew his brains out with his service revolver. He was only 30 years old. That can happen when you lose your ability to smile.

CHAPTER 13

HELLOOOOO FEDERAL

The golden rays caressed her lush body like a lover's embrace. A blonde thatch of hair cascaded down her back like a waterfall of spun silk. Sergeant Hendley had seen her before, sunbathing on the lawn of the Village Apartments. Terri England was an Amazonian beauty, all 6 feet tall of her. She had pale blue eyes and perfect teeth, the most physically perfect woman Hendley had ever seen. He had met her briefly some time back at her place of employment, the Federal Express complex in Franklinville.

He had gone there on a routine call. There was an alarm activation at Federal and the police requested one of our cars respond as theirs were tied up. Hendley was in Car 27 when he received the call. Upon his arrival it was ascertained an accidental alarm and Hendley turned to leave and report via his radio. That's when the "vision" passed by him through the exit door, a girl that made Bo Derek look like "Tugboat Boat Annie". The sergeant attempted to say something to her. He smiled, but before he could open his mouth, she slammed the door in his face. Hendley's pride took a hit. As he stepped into the sunshine, Hendley saw her backing out of a nearby parking space. He had seen her sleek little convertible around town before. The sergeant hastened to jot down the plate number, so he could get a make on the driver back at headquarters. It came back as "Terri England, Apt. 16B, Village Apartments, Southbrook, ILL". It would be a matter of time before their paths crossed again in a small community, and Hendley knew he would exact his revenge for this snobbishness.

And now, there she was in all her glory, sunbathing in a red string that passed as a bikini. On previous "sightings", he had been with someone in the patrol car, but this time he was alone. The plot had been hatching in his mind and was ready for action! As she lay sleeping on her stomach, Hendley eased the car up quietly as near to her as possible. Then, shutting off his engine, the car coasted almost beside her prone figure. The maneuver so far was a success, as she did not stir. Hendley observed, in a rather detached manner, that something else was detached, the top of her bikini. He smiled inwardly as he executed his nefarious scheme.

He picked up his microphone and flipped on the car's overhead speaker system. He then set the volume all the way up and spoke: "HELLOOOOO FEDERAL!"

The startled young woman, still groggy from sleep, jumped up before she realized the top half of her bikini did not follow. She immediately belly-flopped back down to reassemble as Hendley gave a little wave, started up the engine and did a quick U-turn out of the lot! He watched as she flailed about on the ground and heard her yell something. It sounded like she was questioning the legitimacy of his birth.

Hendley later summed up the incident for me in the famous paraphrased words of Sir Winston Churchill:

"NEVER HAS SO PLENTY SHOWN SO MUCH TO SO FEW!"

He nailed Churchill!

CHAPTER 14

SHOOT OUT AT THE OK CORRAL

A cop always remembers the first time he or she has to draw a weapon in the line of duty. Much like remembering your first lover. August 1978 passed without incident, almost. It was the last Friday of the month. Friday around town was normally "hell night". This is the time when the local "gin mills" keep the police busiest. I was riding with Patrolman Proshaska. LoSanta was working the desk that night as he had some "homework" to catch up. LoSanta was studying for his Associates Degree in Criminal Justice, this, despite the Chief.

We were sitting in Unit 18 when I heard a series of sharp loud "pops" through the open window. "Those sounded like shots!" I remarked. I strained to get a fix on the direction. "Naw, probably a car backfiring", said Prohaska. "Not six times in rapid succession", I rebuffed. "Start the unit and let's drift down to Ford St." Judging from the direction of the sound, the only place I could think that would have that kind of action was the "Animal House". That bar is the scene of some of the ugliest incidents I have ever witnessed as a police officer. In the last year alone, there had been nearly a hundred reports requiring police intervention. Yet, its liquor license remained unblemished. It was run by the Mayor of the Boro and a collection of misanthropes we called "The Wild Bunch". That contingent included close relatives of the Chief of Police. Some officers saw fit to "look the other way" when they responded to calls there, even going so far as to make vague logbook entries, no names of course.

As the patrol car made its way down Ford Street, the radio came alive:" shots fired in the Animal House parking lot, Code 3." A Code 3 was the euphemism for "Make a hell of a lot of noise with lights and siren and hope the sons-of-bitches take the hint and run before you arrive!" With shots having been fired, that was okay by me! Prohaska didn't waste a minute hitting the "reds" and "wailers".

Up to this time, I had been remarkably calm; that is, until a nasty thought intruded my consciousness...." suppose that moron doesn't take the hint? If he's drunk, he may not do the rational thing. Here we will be rolling into that lot, lit up like a Christmas tree with holstered weapons. Sitting ducks. For all we knew that "wimp" could be armed with an M16 and was looking down the sites of its barrel awaiting our grand entrance."

Now I was nervous. I unholstered my weapon and held it down by my side. It was the first time it had come out in the line of duty. I put my right hand on the door handle and told Prohaska to put on his high beams. He had already done so. If the gunman is waiting, we could at least blind him temporarily before trying to resolve the situation. I also made a snap decision. If we drew fire or encountered the suspect with the weapon pointed at us, I was going to do my damn to kill him. For a reasonably conservative guy, who was only 15 years ago buying "Pagan Babies" in Catholic School, it was one hell of a decision! But I knew some cops who had been killed going into a life and death situation without first making such a decision, and it was not going to happen to me!

Apparently Prohaska had the same thought. As we hit the lot, he brought the car around to a fast half, and we simultaneously sort of half rolled out of the car, using the doors as frontal shields. We quickly surveyed the shooting scene. A patron of the bar slowly came out from behind a parked car to our front. "He ran away, officers", pointing to the back of the lot. "Look at what he did to my Cadillac!" The man pointed to the holes in the trunk of the white Seville. I slowly walked over to him and counted six holes in the car. Both Prohaska and I were relieved the shooter was not hanging around for any sort of confrontation. As we moved to the read of the lot, we were joined by Patrolman LoSanta. The three of us were standing there when we saw another person running toward us down the side street that ran alongside the lot. As he ran under a streetlight, we recognized a familiar face. It was "Stucky" Stewart, a regular on the Boro bar scene. Breathlessly, he hollered out to us, "He ran that way",, pointing up the street toward Raceway Ave. "Did he still have a gun?" LoSanta asked. "Yeah, I think so", Steward said. "Looked like a small automatic."

Prohaska turned toward the car and motioned me to follow. "LoSanta will go up Raceway Ave. on foot, we will head him off in the car", he said as we jumped in. We paralleled the suspected route of the fleeing felon up Ford Street. "I think it would have been quicker to follow his route up Raceway", I commented in an off-hand manner. "Naw, it's better if we head him off." Prohaska replied.

After a minute, as we neared the border of the Boro, I said, "When the hell are you going to turn off?" We had by this time covered six blocks.   The way Prohaska was procrastinating, you'd think we were pursuing "machine-gun Kelly".   Finally, Prohaska made the turn.   We intersected Raceway Ave and doubled back toward the scene of the shooting. In front of the school we spotted LoSanta coming the other way. "See anything?" I asked. "Nope, I think he ducked in behind the school." LoSanta said.

I wondered about Prohaska's path of pursuit. If we had one after the perpetrator directly, we may have caught him. I couldn't help but wonder if he realized this. LoSanta went back to headquarters to summon the detective bureau, while we attempted to search the wooded area behind the school. I brought the car around back of the school and trained the high beams and spotlight on the woods. Prohaska went in to try and flush him out. I kept the spotlight moving just ahead of him as he searched the woods. I began to feel uneasy again. Should this gunman decide to work around the back of the patrol car, his automatic would put my six-shoot .38 at a distinct disadvantage in terms of firepower. Some of the "autos" could carry up to 15-shot magazines and I carried only five shells in my chamber. The hammer always rested on an empty chamber ever since a cop named Jack Carmel put a bullet in his own leg. It happened during a routine weapons inspection. When he holstered his weapon after the "Present Arms", the hammer caught on the open safety strap and fell on a loaded chamber. Jack lost two toes and went into early retirement.

I hit the electrical switch that released the cr shotgun. The riot gun fell easily into my hands. I depressed the safety button and chambered a round of "00" buckshot. Now I felt a bit more secure.

It was deathly still on this moonless night. Just the chirps of the crickets could be heard. I continued playing the light in front of Prohaska. The minutes ticked by, each one seeming an eternity. As I temporarily lost sight of him in a dense thicket, I heard his voice on the walkie-talkie, "I've got our little night visitor…we're coming out." I uttered a tremendous sign of relief from my entire body.

Prohaska came out of the woods, holding the suspect in front of him. I put the shotgun on the front seat and joined him with my handcuffs. "He says he hid the gun somewhere between the scene and the school", Prohaska informed me. I tucked our suspect into the rear of the car and asked my sidekick to hand me the shotgun. "Be careful", I admonished, "it's loaded and has a hair trigger". I thought I'd mention that to him as the muzzle was pointed to my side of the car. He picked up the weapon, looked at it, pointed it up and pulled the trigger. Nothing happened. I opened my eyes. Prohaska laughed at the expression on my face. "I don't care how hairy this trigger is. You can't fire it unless you manually depress the second safety near the trigger!" One of the few times in my life I've been speechless. The damn thing had double safeties, one to load, one to fire.

"You mean that all the while I was crouching on my smug ass, behind the car, I could NOT have fired that shotgun?" "Nope, not unless you pushed that second button!" Prohaska smiled. I could see he was enjoying this. When he was in a good mood, he would light up one of those stinky little Italian cigars that would make me want to puke. He was reaching for his cigar now. For two years, I had been riding that patrol car and you'd think that someone would have thought to inform me of that double safety feature!

Upon further observation the following day, it was revealed that only two of the seven of the regularly used special police officers we had, knew about the double safety feature. Even more unsettling, two regulars on the force did not know of them. No one had ever fired the shotgun on the shooting range. Another "small" training oversight of our Chief.

Well, I was determined to correct that oversight. The next week, new orders were posted. A "Special Weapons Familiarization Class" was to be held at the firing range and all were required to attend. Shotguns, M1-A3 Carbine, Tear Gas and Machine Guns were to be fired. The latter was an antique, bequeathed to our department from the Dillinger Gang.

What occurred during that class made "Custer's Last Stand" look like a successful military operation.

CHAPTER 15

HOME, HOME ON THE RANGE

Sunday, September 9, 1978. 7 a.m. on a beautiful peaceful day. Someone had hung a picture of the Chief over a target bullseye, and Millstone was emptying a full carbine clip into the shredded image. Qualification day had begun on a positive note. All weapons were aligned on the bench, Reising machine gun, shotguns, carbines and teargas gun. The goal for the day was familiarization with police weaponry, I did spot some out-of-place weapons such as a German Luger, a 1903 Springfield rifle and a Japanese "Arasaka" sniper rifle. They were diplomatically removed by the special officer from whose private collection they had come. The riddled picture of the Chief was laid to rest in a trash container and the serious business got under way.

Above five minutes into orientation, performed by Sergeants Salterella and Millstone, a familiar voice sounded across the encampment. It was the Chief. "I don't want any man getting hurt! And everyone will pick up their 'brass' and 'police' the range. I want everything left neat and clean, clean and neat!" Oh well, so much for a peaceful day, I thought to myself.

Chief Wildman stood with arms folded across his chest at the back of the seated men. The range personnel had selected the Reising machine gun as the first weapon. As a clip of ammunition was inserted into the antique, the Chief sauntered up to the head of the class and took the weapon from the instructors. We all shuttered. The class was being lectured on the firing characteristics of the Reising. We were being warned of its tendency to go up when firing a long burst. "Fire short bursts", Millstone had warned. The admonition did not make an impression on the Chief. After all, he knew all about such trivialities. He would show the boys how it was to

67

be fired. The Chief pointed the weapon up range, cocked the gun and pulled the trigger. True to its nature, the prolonged burst brought the barrel up. Despite a deep earthen backdrop behind the targets, we heard the distinctive "clink" of metal hitting metal, down range. Some rounds had hit the Canal Bridge 200 yards behind the targets.

As luck would have it, no cars were crossing the bridge at that time of morning. The Chief led a charmed life. Just one car hit by one stray bullet and our beloved Chief's career would have ended. I envisioned the morning headline: 'POLICE CHIEF ACCIDENTALLY MACHINE GUNS CARLOAD OF CHURCH GOERS!" Nothing fatal, mind you, just one little hole in a fender or trunk. The officers around me were in stitches. Patrolman Elders called out, "We think we heard something hit the bridge yonder Chief!" Wildman turned to Millstone and asked the officer if he heard anything. Millstone took the ear plug out of his good ear and said "Eh?" Most of us were in spasms now. I got out of there before I wet my pants. I walked back off the firing line and had a cigarette.

The remainder of the morning was relatively uneventful. Sgt. Hendley, on the rebound from an all-nighter, shook so badly he failed to qualify. The Chief of the Auxiliary Police was thrown off the range for pointing a weapon back toward the firing line (a definite no-no on any range). Also, the cable suspending the targets had been shot down three times.

By late afternoon, the final event was taking place. The familiarization and firing of the teargas gun. As the Range Officer was issuing the final instruction, the Chief re-appeared. Wildman took it upon himself to address the group as the first volunteer to fire the gun. I slipped up beside Salterella, "Vince, do you think it's wise, based on this morning's fiasco, letting the Chief fire the teargas?" Vince looked at me and said in a resigned tone, "No, but then, who the hell is going to tell him that?" I nodded in acknowledgement and sat down for the inevitable climax of the day.

Officer Millstone was explaining that the weapon should always be fired at a slight angle, in effect, lobbing the canister from the muzzle of the gun. We could tell the Chief hadn't listened to a word of instruction, as he had been off to the side chatting with another person. The time came to actually fire the gun. The Range Officers had elected to discharge the weapon into the river alongside our range so that the water would nullify the effect of the gas. Also, the wind, though somewhat variable that day, was blowing away from the group. The Chief brought the stock of the weapon to his shoulder, elevated the barrel and fired. A loud bang, and the canister load gracefully arched its way to its landing site. Alas, too little heading and too much elevation, and the barrel was too high. The canister cleared the narrow river and canal and landed on a main street of our neighbor, Eastbrook.

As a cloud of tear gas rose from the opposite shore, the Chief heard a commotion behind him. Lowering the barrel of the gun, he turned around. All he saw were cars speeding out of the parking lot. Not a solitary person was left behind. As I depressed the pedal on the accelerator, I glanced back through the rear window. A figure in blue stood alone, with a nebulous cloud rapidly drifting toward his back. I laughed out loud. Who says there's no justice? The wind had shifted, and the gas was blowing back toward our range....and Chief Wildman.

CHAPTER 16

WE ALWAYS GET OUR MAN

The cold winds of winter were starting to blow. It was unusually cold for early November. I was back behind the desk, wishing I had a job assignment in the warm climate of Florida. The front page of the news had its usual photo of some scantily clad nymphet posing on the beach in Ft. Lauderdale. I knew it was going to be Winter soon when I saw that "stock" photo pose, revealing some far-off Chamber of Commerce.

Patrol Officers LoSanta and Prohaska were working the streets in Units 27 and 28. The ring of the telephone interrupted my obscene thoughts of the smiling Surf Queen. The clock read midnight. A male caller informed me that his parked car had just been struck on Edgemere Rd. by a hit-and-run driver. The man described the vehicle as an orange pickup with a white camper body. I alerted the patrol cars to the event and the description of the pickup. I started a log entry of the event, when LoSanta called over the radio, "Car 27 to 699, am in pursuit of suspect vehicle, westbound on Edgemere." LoSanta could be depended on for fast results.

Despite his outward slow manner, LoSanta had one of the sharpest minds in the department. His thin angular features and slow wide grin which crossed his face from ear to ear, earned him the nickname "Howdy Doody". The name was pinned on him by a drunk out-of-state driver, who remarked that he bore resemblance to the puppet. LoSanta also bore the scars of conflict with the Chief. Only his were more psychological than physical. The running feuds between the two left LoSanta very bitter and disillusioned.

LoSanta and Prohaska had caught the suspect and pulled him over, but not before the driver had jumped a curb, run over a lawn, coming to rest against a small fence. "Both cars will be out in front of 161 Height St. Request a 'Hook' at said location." I put in a call for a tow truck from headquarters. A few minutes had passed before I heard from the patrols. Prohaska broke the silence and radioed they were coming to headquarters to administer a breathalyzer, a machine that chemically analyzes a suspected drunk driver's alcohol intake. For some undetermined reason, there was an undercurrent of mirth in Prohaska's voice, the kind of tone you get when you pick up the phone after enjoying a good joke.

Both officers were smiling broadly when they ushered in the suspect through the rear door of the station. "Guess who we have here?" Prohaska announced in a triumphant voice. "J. Edgar Hoover, drunk driving", I replied sarcastically. "No, someone more important to me", Prohaska explained. "I got Chiggers". It was my turn to start grinning. The legend of Chiggers was well-known in headquarters. He was the Councilman who cast the tie-breaking vote to elect Chief Wildman twenty years ago. Passing over the then Detective Sergeant, who was senior man in the department and the most logical choice. The detective, bitter and disillusioned about that political decision, resigned from the force. That detective was none other than Prohaska. He came back to the only life he knew after his business failed and started all over again as a patrolman under the leadership of the man he despised. Now the man who gave us Wildman stood arrested by the officer whom he screwed out of fifteen years as a cop. Fate does work in strange ways.

As Chiggers walked past my desk, mumbling incoherently, I noticed an ungodly odor. As he walked, he left a trail of brown spots in his wake. He was defecating in his pants and it was travelling down his pant leg. I was overcome with a sense of revulsion at the stench. Prohaska saw my expression and interjected, "That's why he was in such a big hurry. The bar closed and he had the runs. He was trying to make it home." I told the officers to administer the test while I went out to get some air. "You think the floors a mess, you should see the back of the patrol car!" "No thanks."

Chiggers failed all the sobriety tests with flying colors. He was promptly booked on a variety of charges. We couldn't find an ordinance to cover defecating in police headquarters or soiling a police car. After the episode, I decided to leave early. Prohaska and LoSanta locked up headquarters to preserve the aroma for the incoming day personnel. Before closing shop, LoSanta smiled that ear-to-ear grin and informed me, "We always get our man." Sometimes it takes a little longer that we'd like. I think he might have seen one too many Canadian Mounties movies, be he had a point.

The stinking floor and the foul patrol car were specifically left for the Chief's early arrival. To make sure he wouldn't miss out on the aroma, we had Chiggers sit in the Chief's office for a little while. After all, to the victor belong the spoils!

CHAPTER 17

HAVE GUN WILL TRAVEL

"Another minute and I could have wasted all you cops!" snarled the biker. Sitting there, handcuffed to the chair, one would have thought the dirt bag would have enough sense to shut-up. He looked as nasty as they come. I eyed him with a certain curiosity, however, as we seldom get them this bad as to be threatened with death. He was tall and wiry, with dirty hair that was shoulder length, and about 3 days' growth on his beard. I nicknamed him "Mazola Head" because of the greasy hair. His black leather jacket had the insignia "Demons", the name of his motorcycle gang.

We had to have "Mazola" at headquarters due to an anonymous telephone call. The caller said that someone was going to sell some guns in the parking lot of the Animal House. I called the detectives and informed them. They put enough stock in it to arrange a stake-out of the lot that night. Detectives Hendershot and Chin parked their unmarked unit in the lot with Patrolman Quinto as backup.

A few minutes past 2 a.m., I heard Hendershot on Channel 3 of the walkie talkie. "The deal is going down. Two suspects near the car with the open trunk. Car 27, move in." I reflected on how happy I was that I got that third channel hookup on the radio. A band like that gave us a private channel to carry out such assignments. We didn't have to use the common channel shared with other locales, especially when criminals were savvy enough to have police scanners.

Car 27 converged with the two detectives and caught a bar patron showing a couple of Smith and Wesson .38's to Mazola Head. Fortunately, they were unloaded. Unfortunately, the bust was premature. The deal had not been consummated. The money and weapons had not changed hands. In the dark parking lot, it was difficult for the detectives to gauge when they should move in. Both suspects were brought to headquarters, and that's when Mazola and I met for the first and last time. There's no doubt in my mind the guy was high on something. His initial comment sort of made me glad the bust hadn't occurred a minute later. I believed what he said about "wasting" cops. I was even madder when Detective Chin told me we had to let him go free. He was "clean" and there were no warrants out on him. Chin's comment to us, however, made me persist. "Isn't there anything we can get him on? Did he litter? Spit on the sidewalk? Anything?" To no avail. The decision had been handed down to "cut him loose".

"Don't worry", Hendershot whispered to me. "I'm not forgetting that comment". The two detectives and myself, advanced toward the suspect to uncuff him. Dequinto had left with the gun seller for County. Mazola, seeing us coming toward him, looked a little worried. "You guys aren't going to play a little Blind Man's Bluff with me, are you?" Blind Man's Bluff, or Pin the Tail on the Donkey, were (by way of explanation), a variation of the childrens games involving a seated suspect under a metal trash barrel while cops circled around him beating the barrel with their nightsticks. The suspect would guess which one hit him. If he succeeded, they stopped the "game". Sometimes. "We don't beat our prisoners in this Boro", Hendershot seemed genuinely insulted. "You are free to go. We will escort you to our County line. We don't ever want to see your face around here again."

Hendershot and Mazola Head left the scene. "How do we know he won't come back? And, what did Hendershot mean about not forgetting that comment?" I asked Chin. In his inscrutable manner, Chin smiled at me and asked, "Did you ever try walking a deserted road late at night, freezing cold weather, with no shoes?" Ah, so, I looked out into the January night air from the back door and pondered this Oriental logic. Mazola Head was never seen or heard from again.

CHAPTER 18

ENTER TONY ROME

Halinger and Elders sped to the location of my dispatch. A squad at the Animal House. A phoned in Code 11, possible cardiac. A patron had suddenly slumped from his stool and had fallen to the floor. Both officers pulled up to the side door with oxygen equipment and waded into the mobbed establishment. The commotion that greeted them made them think how appropriately named was this place. They could hardly hear themselves ask for directions to the location of the stricken person. "Please, make room", they pled, and they pushed and shoved their way toward him. The victim was already quite blue when they got to him. Halinger opened the oxygen and put the mask to the gentleman's face. This would aid him until the rescue squad arrived on the scene.

Within minutes, the squad pulled up, met with the same wall-to-wall mob. Cameron was less prone to be polite than the other officers, and forcefully shoved his way through the mass. "The oxygen isn't doing him any good", he's still having trouble breathing", Elders remarked. Cameron knelt beside the victim and ripped the oxygen mask away. Peering down the stricken's man throat, Cameron stuck his fingers into the mouth and reached down his air pipe and extracted a half-chewed piece of food. "No wonder the oxygen didn't do any good, asshole, the guy was choking to death!" Cameron lambasted the two embarrassed officers. "Now, give him the damn oxygen!" They readied him to be removed to the hospital. It wasn't going to be easy, however. Some of the patrons who were shoved out of the way took umbrage with Cameron's gruff manner. They refused to let the squad take the victim to the ER. The two policemen attempted to aid but were powerless against the some 200 or more "inmates" of the Animal House. When some of them grabbed beer bottles, the threat was substantial enough for Cameron to call for assistance over his radio. Elders and Halinger would be of little help given the crowd. Enter Tony Rome.

As both road officers were on the scene, I radioed Eastbrook Police for backup. I recognized the voice of the responding officer, sending a shiver up my spine. Tony's booming voice almost jarred me out of my chair. The Animal House was about to receive its due reward.

The only way to describe Tony's physical appearance is he was built roughly like a cube, as wide as he was high, and every inch pure mean. The local guys nicknamed him "Mongo" after the guy that knocked out the horse in "Blazing Saddles". The movie's Mongo was almost as mean as Tony. Officer Rome's reputation as quashing bar disturbances was local legend. The hospital should have an orthopedic ward dedicated to Tony, as he continuously challenged bone doctors with a plethora of ways to break bones. Tony opened the door to Animal House and walked into midst of the confrontation. One of the less sober patrons stood in Tony's way. The man had overheard our call for help and was surprised when only one officer showed up. With his companion's support, the drunk was reasonably sure of himself in saying, "Shit man, only one…" The sentence was never completed. Officer Rome picked him up and threw him about ten feet. He sailed completely over the bar into the display of bottles. It looked like "Godzilla vs. Kermit the Frog". Out came Tony's lead sap. Two more anti-socials hit the bar floor before the idea spread that this guy was not there for the bar's pepperoni pizza! A clear path materialized in front of Tony and the rescue squad. Cameron quickly got his patient out on the dolly. The joint was quiet now as Tony addressed the throng. "I'm closing this gin-mill right now. Everyone out!" Without so much as a whimper from the bartenders, the place was cleared out. It was said that one guy opted to leave by the bathroom window rather than take the time to locate a door.

The next day, the Dwarf (owner of the Animal House), came into headquarters upset about the forced closing, especially since it was ordered who was not even a member of our department. He was told to take his complaint across the river to Eastbrook's Police Department. Tony was working at the time and after witnessing what he had done the previous night, I would have driven him there personally.

CHAPTER 19

THE UNARREST

The shenanigans at Animal House continued to worsen. The officers in our department were instructed to keep close watch, especially the parking lot. Halinger and I were working car 27 when we got a call of a disturbance in the lot.

As we rolled into the lot, we saw a crowd gathered around a person standing atop a parked car. Actually, "standing" was is not the right word, he was jumping up and down on the roof of a parked car. We could hear some of the gathering spectators pleading with the man to get down. When we pushed our way through the circle of people, the beam of my flashlight lit up the defiant subject. It was the Chief's nephew, Joey Wildman.

Obviously intoxicated, flailing his arms about and cursing, he was about to topple of his own accord we didn't get to him soon. It was determined from those around that the car was not owned by the man atop, who was attempting to lower the roof into the chassis. After all, there's no law that says you can't destroy our own property, only that of another. In short, we had him "by the balls", and I for was, not going to let go.

I asked a superfluous question of my partner, "shall we take him in?" His response was, "Take in Joey? Naw, I want no problems. Let's just get him down and settle this matter between the owner of the car and Joey. If the owner wants to sign a complaint tomorrow, we'll be around." On the surface, his response seemed reasonable enough, but I had seen this ploy in operation before. Technically, the senior officer could sign a complaint, as the lieutenant saw an actual witness to the perpetration. By allowing the civilian to make the complaint the next day, the time lapse would allow peculiar things to happen. It would be made known to the complainant that if we swore out a warrant, a counter-complaint would certainly follow with a few well-chosen false witnesses to add validity to the counter charges. He kinship to the Chief would also be made known for further leverage. The charges were inevitably dropped, and a cash settlement made. How one puts a cash value on damaged eyes, lacerated faces and broken bones was anyone's guess. It worked time and time again for the keepers of the Animal House.

Lieutenant Halinger grabbed at Joey Wildman's foot in an attempt to dislodge him from the car roof. It worked. Joey lost his balance and fell on top of Halinger. It looked like "King Kong" falling off the Empire State Building on top of Woody Allen. Both subjects sprawled to the ground. Halinger's composure began to unravel. What Joey did next finished the process. He jumped up and as Halinger was attempting to rise, gave him a little push. It was as though he was possibly attempting to steady himself rather than a blatant act against Halinger. The effect was the same though, as Halinger fell backward on the ground.

Then it happened. A miracle! Not a minor miraculous event such as making the lame walk, the blind see or the dumb speak, but a cataclysmic event on par with Moses parting the Red Sea. Halinger arrested Joey Wildman! I stood there astonished, unable to comprehend what had just befallen our Boro. Jesus! He had arrested the Chief's nephew...." No problem"...Halinger had just done what no other copy in town would have even thought of doing, and I had witnessed it.

Albeit a minor transgression, Joey was charged with simple assault under a Boro statute, (a similar charge under a State statute would have meant jail time). I had the arrest card made out before Halinger had finished writing out the summons back at headquarters. It was to make sure there was no turning back for him. I could see Halinger wavering already, sweating, pulling at his tie and cuffs, pacing back and forth, all the signs of fear and remorse setting in on him. Only on him, it looked like signs of advanced rigor mortis. When I handed him the arrest card, he saw his name stood out in capital letters: ARRESTING OFFICER, LT. K. HALINGER!

The coffin was nailed shut! There was no turning back now. His eyes wide, he exclaimed, "Dammit! Did you have to fill out that card so fast?" "Isn't that usual procedure?" I asked innocently. "When one arrests a person, an arrest card is to be made out." Halinger did not answer.

I began to fantasize. All the surrounding police departments would want framed copies when the arrest became public. I could see that arrest card in the foyers of all the local departments with "appropriate" captions. To paraphrase an old saying, "The moving finger of fate…. having written….and all your weeping cannot erase a single word."

Halinger sat down at the desk to write the police logbook entry. After he was finished, I glanced at the entry as I was curious as to what he had written. The Entry read as follows:

"ARREST, SIMPLE ASSAULT, 11:00 P.M., MONDAY MARCH 1ST. Lieutenant Halinger and Deputy Castle responded to parking of lot of local establishment to investigate report of disturbance. Altercation ensued and, arrested for simple assault on the person of a police officer was one Jake Whitman…."

I read no further. Wait a minute…the name on the blotter hit me between the eyes. Jake Whitman? "Who the hell is Jake Whitman?" In inquired of the Lieutenant. Halinger began what at first resembled the mating dance of the Crested Whooping Crane. "God dammit, you know good and well who you arrested out there!" I could feel the hot stabs of anger in my voice, "and it wasn't any Jake Whitman!" His lame retort was "That's the name that I thought the subject had given." "Look, you know, and I know who was arrested." Any icy edge crept into my voice…" either you correct that entry or I'll have YOU up on charges for falsifying an official police document!" I really had no idea if I could or not, but the threat was enough to collapse his attempted sham. He sat down and corrected the log.

Just to be certain, I made copies of the arrest card should the original mysteriously "disappear". Before leaving, I dropped one into the Chief's mail slot. There's nothing like starting the morning off with a bang! Especially in this case, where the bang being heard would be the sound of the Chief's head hitting the ceiling of his office.

The court date fell on the second Tuesday of March. As I was working the desk that evening, I requested Hendershot let me know what transpired. The three local newspapers were always represented at court, so the case would certainly get some press coverage.

The appointed evening session of court went rather slowly. At 11 p.m. Hendershot came back into headquarters. I was questioning him before he had the front door shut. "What happened", I asked. "Nothing". "What? What do you mean 'nothing'. Something had to happen!" Hendershot looked as bewildered as I. "Nothing happened because the case never came up", he said. The detective went on to explain that when the case did not come up, he went to the clerk and asked to see the docket of scheduled cases. The "Joey Wildman" case was not on the docket. It was postponed or rescheduled, the court clerk did not even have a copy of the summons. The case had simply vanished. Hendershot summed it up in these words, "The defendant was UNARRESTED".

Unarrested? Now that's a new word in judicial procedure. "How the Hell can someone be unarrested?" I asked the detective. He shrugged his shoulders in resignation. "In this town, anything can happen". He was right. In this town, anything could and did happen, including unarrests.

CHAPTER 20

HENDLEY GETS "MOONED"

The "Moonies" were in town. Like the flowers in Spring that bring forth their blossoms, the disciples of the Reverend Sun-Yung Moon bloomed in Southbrook. Cameron, Hendley and myself were working an otherwise quiet Sunday afternoon shift in May of 1979. Our headquarters had received numerous complaints in reference to the pesky devotees of the Reverend, soliciting from door-to-door. "Why don't they stay where they belong, blocking the ramps of the airports?" Cameron had reflected after reading the daily reports.

Before he left in the patrol car, I reminded Hendley, if he should encounter any "bald-headed ascetics" in long robes, to check them to see if they had permits to solicit as required by our Boro ordinances. Hendley, his usual rough Saturday night behind him, nodded briskly as he went out the door. With Cameron in Car 28 and Hendley in 27 on the road, I got down to some serious police business...reading Cameron's "Hustler" magazine. (I never knew whipped cream could be used in so many 'delicious' ways).

Unknown to us at the station, another event was taking place that would alter our otherwise blissful Sunday. A building dedication was taking place just across the boundary line in Franklinville. The Japanese firm, Tanaka, was opening a branch of its facilities that afternoon. As is their custom, a contingent of Buddhist Monks was to be present to bless the new venture. Somehow the carload lost their direction and stopped at a home on our main street to get directions. About the time they were knocking on a door, Hendley wheeled Car 27 around a corner and caught sight of the group. Hendley pulled up to the bald-headed priests in their bright orange robes and stepped out of the car. "Alright, you people, where's your permit to solicit?" Hendley inquired. Not have a solid command of the English language, they smiled and bowed low as is their custom, but said nothing. A leader stepped forward. "Where…. Tanaka?" he asked. The sergeant replied that he knew no one named Tanaka in the Boro. Again, Hendley asked for a permit and got the same reply. Seeing he was getting nowhere with his line of questioning, Hendley decided to adjourn to the stationhouse which was only a block away. (Everything in our small Boro is a block away). The officer motioned to the group to follow his lead. Whether it was his official uniform or the impression that they were going to be taken to "Tanaka", the group followed Hendley down the street.

The sight of this police officer at the head of a parade of bald orange-robed Asians marching down the main street of our town must have been quite something to see. With their brass bells tinkling as they went, it must have resembled an Asian version of the Pied Piper. Into the police station Hendley and his "Merry Men" came. That's where I saw them for the first time. "Here's your bald Asiatics that have been soliciting", Hendley announced triumphantly. Holding back the laughter that was welling up inside, I put my hand on the sergeant's shoulder in consolation. "I said BALD ASCETICS, NOT ASIATICS!". "The Moonies are Caucasian US persons, not Asiatics. What you have brought me are Buddhist Monks!"

Hendley was as confused as the rest of us at this point. "Are you sure?" he asked me. "I'm sure", was the reply, "I've seen enough of them in Japan to distinguish Monks from Moonies!"

The spokesperson again stepped forward and asked, "Tanaka?" The question was beginning to take a significance similar to "Rosebud" of "Citizen Kane". I suddenly remembered something I had heard over the police radio on a special detail that Franklinville was setting up for that day. Something about a dedication of a new building in their industrial campus. On a hunch, I called Franklinville headquarters and asked the name of the new company. Their response…" Tanaka". Case solved!

CHAPTER 21

CREEPING TOM

The usual calls regarding "Peeping Toms" are, for the most part, harmless. With the advent of Cable TV and accompanying uncut movies, these types have calls have been reduced to almost nothing. The majority of "Tom" calls are more fantasy than fact. An example that comes to mind is the call we received from the "Fenwick Funny Farm". The woman caller reported a "Peeping Tom" looking into her third story window. They must have been a human fly, since there were no fire escapes on her side of the building. We also got a report from a male caller reporting a female "Peeping Tomasina", though just what the Hell he was complaining about I'll never know.

The one case of this sort that does merit retelling is the incident that occurred on the night of June 17, l979. I dispatched officer Tom (appropriately named) Wallerstein to investigate a report of a "Creeping Tom". The caller reported a man crawling on her front porch and looking into her bedroom window. The officer was met at the door by an irate, but voluptuous blonde in her early twenties. "My friends call me Zip, officer." The robe she wore left little to the imagination. As she gave the details of the event, she nervously cinched the robe she wore, causing the top to bow slightly. Officer Wallerstein caught his breath. "I'll check around outside and be right back", he stated, as he went out to check the area. "Good", she replied. "I'll go throw something on while you're gone."

A check of the grounds produced nothing, and Wallerstein reclimbed the steps to the porch to knock on the door. At this time, he noticed the window to her bedroom. It was one of those older types that sent almost from floor to ceiling. The shades to the room were up and the curtains drawn. She was in the process of "throwing something on". Tom later mused at headquarters, "It looked like she almost missed." Wallerstein shook his head in disbelief, as he knocked on the door and was let back in. The officer reported he had seen nothing outside and took out his notepad for a preliminary report. Zip began her story. "Well, I had gotten home late and went to my bedroom to change, when…." The officer interrupted her. "Were the drapes drawn or the shade pulled down?" She thought a moment before replying. "Well, no…but…". Wallerstein broke in, "You mean that you undressed in front of this huge window that provided an unobstructed view to your activities to anyone passing by on the street?" The young lady was silent. Putting his pad and pen aside, Wallerstein told the woman that in the future, before disrobing, she should pull down the shade and/or draw the curtains. "It would go a long way toward discouraging Peeping and Creeping Toms", he chided. Warning her to be more careful in the future, Tom Wallerstein opened the front door and walked to his car. As he reached the door, he heard squeaking from across the street. He observed an elderly man, about 70, sitting on the front porch. The streetlight made the man discernable as he rocked back and forth in his rocking chair. From his vantage point, Wallerstein noted that the man's white pants were dirty around the knees. The officer called out, "Did you ever hear the story of Lady Godiva and Peeping Tom?" "Nope, don't believe I've heard that one", the old man replied.

Believing his point to be made, Wallerstein smiled and got into the car. "30 to headquarters for a report", he gunned the vehicle into the quiet summer evening.

CHAPTER 22

ROCKY RACCOON TAKES SIX IN THE BELLY

Hendley had an almost tragic accident. While pursuing a suspect who was wanted for "bouncing" checks, he crashed through the glass front doors of the Pussycat Motel. We at headquarters assumed he was there in the line of duty. The sergeant was acting on a "stop and hold" order from Franklinville. The subject in question bolted when the officer attempted to question him and ran through the open entrance door. The doors to the establishment were controlled by an automatic device, the kind that activate the door when you step on the carpet. Hendley started after the person through the same door, which swung closed on him just as he got to the doorway. He ran full tilt into the glass pane. Stunned, Hendley fell to the carpet, bleeding from a severe laceration of his gun hand. It took 30 stitches to close the wound.

The sergeant and I were working the midnight shift, his first tour of duty since the accident. His hand still bandaged, "dead eyes", as Cameron called him, was working the patrol car and I, the desk. About an hour into our shift, I received a call, referring to a hurt or sick raccoon lying in the roadway of Water Street. I dutifully radioed Hendley to check it out, cautioning him as we had had reports of rabid animals in the vicinity.

This summer night was peaceful and quiet. At least it was, until I heard a rapid succession of gunfire reverberating through the night air. The phone console lit up like a nymphomaniac at a stag party on Alcatraz. One call after another about the shots. Suspecting Hendley had something to do with it, as the calls were in the proximity of Water Street, I called the sergeant, "Are you aware of the gunshot reports?" "Affirmative", replies he. "I had to put the animal out of his misery?" I asked him if it was necessary to use the machine gun at 1 a.m. to kill the animal. He did not reply. I requested he 30 to headquarters.

Upon his arrival, Hendley strode to the desk and dropped six empty shell casings on the glass top. As they clattered around, he opened his service revolver and proceeded to extract six more empties. "What the hell you shoot at out there, King Kong?" I laughed. The dialogue continued.

"Twelve bullets to kill a raccoon?"

"He was moving".

"How far away was this animal?"

"About 2 feet away".

"You were 2 feet away from the animal, lying in the street, and it took 12 shots to kill it?"

"My gun hand is still stiff from the accident."

By this time, Hendley was getting irritated with the questioning. He attempted to justify his inaccuracy by elaborating further, "I was using wad-cutter (target) ammo to reduce ricochets and the animal was moving!" When he saw me shaking my head with laughter, he knew further dialogue was useless and left headquarters to resume his patrol.

I wrote up a bogus police report on the incident and posted it on the bulletin board for the day shift. It read as follows:

SUBJECT: DOA, gunshot wounds

NAME: Rocky, Raccoon

AGE: N/A

SEX: Not anymore

RACE: Black

INV/OFF: Sgt. Hendley

"Masked" perpetrator attempted to flee investigating officer Hendley. In ensuing gunfire, Mr. Raccoon died of fright after having been shot at twelve times by the officer, Sergeant Hendley, escaped with minor abrasions to his ego. Corpus Delecti of victim turned over the ASPCA for an autopsy to determine cause of death. --- J. J. Castle, Desk Officer

CHAPTER 23

DESIREE IN THE DUST

I never thought of the possibility that a pistol qualification exercise might become a sexual fantasy. That is, not until I met Desiree O'Brien.

I had brought my special and auxiliary police officers to the Franklinville shooting range as part of their semi-annual qualifications for bearing sidearms. Instead of the normal yearly tactical revolver course demanded of regular police officers. I had made in mandatory for the men under my jurisdiction to qualify twice a year. Once a year, they would qualify on our smaller more informal range, and once a year they would participate with the Franklinville specials on their range. It was run more professionally and was larger and more difficult than our course. This year Franklinville had added something to their range obstacles – Desiree.

She was, in every way, a "special" officer. Her lush figure strained at the seams of her tailored uniform. Of Irish descent, Desiree's dark hair and flawless creamy-white skin and green eyes did to my men what years of training attempted to subvert. To wit, she turned them into gaping, sweaty-palmed adolescents. Unfortunately, she had the same effect on me.

The Range Officer in charged "buddied" up to the officers of the two departments. An officer of Franklinville would team up with a Southbrook officer, one would act as aide to the other and then the roles would be reversed. Fate selected Desiree and me to be a team. Desiree O'Brien and Deputy Director Castle. It sounded good over the public address announcement. My men looked at me as if I had shot their mothers. I instinctively knew what they were thinking. "Aha! The fix was in. Rank has its privileges." Fact was, I thought it was the worst possible pairing. Sort of having paired Dolly

Parton and Twiggy in a wet T-shirt competition. If there was one person I didn't want to be "buddied" up to, it was Desiree. Attending to the difficult business at hand would be made more difficult with her nearby. I was attempting to figure out a way to get out of the predicament in diplomatic fashion, when I hear that soft voice of my partner behind me. "It looks like you and I are together today, Jay." Her voice had all the intimacy of an X-rated movie. I turned slowly and as met with a dazzling smile of perfect teeth molded into a face, and a frame that Racquel Welch would envy. Looking at her, I mentally thanked God for not having an officer like her on my roster. Every red-blooded male over the age of puberty would have clamored to carry a badge in our town. In addition to trying to keep Officer Elders away from her, the jealous wives and fistfights of those who wished to share a patrol car with her, would have been some job in itself! I'd have to have a patrol car guarding her patrol car.

I squeaked a reply to her greeting, and we walked to the firing line together. At least I walked, she did something else that resembled locomotion. Whatever it was, I wouldn't call it walking. I heard a few moans behind us as we progressed to our assigned positions. We received our allotment of practice rounds to fire for familiarization. With Desiree at my elbow, I fired my first shots. "Your hand is shaking", Desiree observed. I'm glad she didn't look at my knees. They weren't doing very well either.

"Here, let me show you how to steady your grip", she volunteered as she moved closer to my arm. The ensuing contact was, I'm sure, accidental. Her breast touched my upper arm. I damn near dropped by .38. It was like an electric shock zapping 600 volts through my being. I regained what was left of my composure as she put both her arms around my extended gun arm. She was explaining something about a two-handed grip, but I didn't hear. The scent of her perfume and her long raven hair, the warmth of her opulent body pressing against my side caused a pounding in my heart that transcended the spoken word.

It was love. I was in love. I was sexually aroused surrounded by 100 police officers. Boy, I sure pick my opportunities carefully. I silently prayed, "Please, Lord, let me concentrate on the silhouette at the end of the range and not the one standing next to me." Despite my plea, Fate had cast the die and they came up "snake eyes".

The first firing position, twelve shots from the prone position, had Desiree lying so close to me on the ground the warmth of her body scorched my Jockeys. With the scent of Chanel No. 5 in my nostrils and the ensuing visual distraction, I completed a shaky qualification. My partner and I walked up range to score my target. I thought I had qualified, even though it would have been a sub-par score. Imagine my surprise when we got to the target and saw it was almost devoid of hits. A glance at the adjoining silhouette told me why. I had lost my concentration on the first position and had shot at the adjoining target. The officer next to me, whose target I peppered, was a novice auxiliary who had shot on a timed range for the first time. He had a score of 280 out of a possible 300. According to the Rules of the Range, my hits on his target counted toward his score. (And, it was impossible to tell which hits were mine). For the first time I had failed to qualify on the range.

As I had qualified on our Boro range, and given the circumstances, I could requalify at a later date. This I did, and without Desiree present, passed the course a week later. It was embarrassing, however, and I took a lot of good-natured kidding. "Hey, Jay, you must have had a tough time firing from the prone next to O'Brien! You should have used her tits as a bench rest!"

Needless to say, Desiree needed a lot of "corrective instruction" when it came her turn to qualify. She shot a 272. Guess I didn't have the same effect on her that she had on me.

I received a good lesson in Constitutional History from her, all people are NOT created equal. It's all a matter of being "endowed".

CHAPTER 24

YELLOW STREAM INCIDENT

Everyone has a pet peeve, (or even hate), and I have a few. My pet peeves are when tearing a piece of paper from a pad, just as you get to the end of the sheet it rips off a jagged hunk from the corner. Another peeve of mine is those people who can belch or pass gas with incessant repetition regardless of social surroundings. My biggest annoyance is cops who refuse to use the "facilities" to urinate, as civil custom dictates.

Prohaska and I were riding together in the marked unit, logging another mundane night into history. My head was dangling out of the car window as his favorite Italian cigar fumigated the car. "Well, at least that thing will keep the mosquitos away", I said aloud. "Eh?", Prohaska responded in his usual loquacious manner. He pushed the pack of black little mummified Denobli's across the top of the dashboard. "Have one.... make a man out of you." "No thanks", I responded quickly. "I hear the Mafia makes them things out of the penises of its victims." Prohaska roared with delight as we turned into the Orthodox Cemetery.

As we passed the well-attended rows of headstones, I was about to ask what the hell we were doing here when Prohaska brought the car to a sudden halt. "What's the matter? You see something?" I asked. "Naw. Got some business to attend to." He left the car. Prohaska was too old to be into necrophilia or too honest for grave robbing, so I couldn't help but wonder what type of business he had in the cemetery at 3 a.m. In the faint moonlight, I watched his approach to a small grove of trees. He stood for a moment, then unzipped his fly and urinated. I thought for a moment he was paying his last respects on Palko's grave.

I sat transfixed as Prohaska got back to the car. "Was *that* the business? Of all the places to piss, you select a cemetery?" I rebuked. "Why didn't we just 30 to headquarters instead of defiling hallowed ground." Prohaska was silent for a moment, then lashed out, "Look! I had to take a leak and this place was convenient, ok?"

I sat silently remembering last year when a patrolman chose to use the side of the school building as a lavatory. A teenage girl rounded the corner and surprised him. He stood, "pecker" in hand as the girl fled screaming. Charges were later brought against the officer by the girl for indecent exposure. He was found guilty, but the girl dropped the complaint when she was assured it would be handled internally. The episode would have cost him his career had it gotten to court.

The next time, I made a mental note, I would do something to prevent Prohaska from repeating his nocturnal emissions outside headquarters. Prohaska was sort of the elder statesman of the force and was well-liked by everybody. Except of course, the Chief, who didn't really like anybody. He would have loved to get something like this on Prohaska.

Toward the end of the following week, Prohaska and I found ourselves sharing a patrol car, as we cruised the naked streets in the early a.m., the church cemetery cropped up on our inspection rounds. It was a full moon when we entered the cemetery. Prohaska's kidneys were baying at the moon as the werewolf urge compelled him to pee in the pale silvery light. A solitary ray of light shone from a window of a home bordering the grounds. "I've got to see a man about a horse". His unoriginal phrase rang in my ears as the car door slammed. The somewhat sinister event that followed perhaps would have made a good TV scene. (better than Gilligan's Island anyhow). Entitled, EMISSION IMPOSSIBLE: (Scene, Bathroom, Man standing over toilet. Voice from tape recorder can be heard to say "Good evening Mr. Phelps.... should you or any of your EMF be caught pissing, the Chief of Police will disavow any connection. This toilet will self-destruct in ten seconds."

Prohaska made his way to his favorite spot. You could tell it was his favorite, as the grass turf had a large dead spot in an otherwise green lush area. The groundskeeper must have been going nuts trying to figure out why the grass was dying in just this one spot. The officer unzipped and commenced to water the grass. That's when I slipped over to the driver's seat and flipped on the powerful spotlight. Its beam caught Prohaska in "midstream". In his haste to retreat, Prohaska soaked the cuff of his trousers and his shoes.

He swore a blue streak at me as he jumped into the patrol car. I remained silent as we drove back to headquarters, presumably to finish what he had started. Sgt. Salterella met us at the back door. "When you have a chance, check out a complaint we got over the telephone. Some guy urinating in the church cemetery. The caller said he lives by the property and saw some guy in what he thought was a uniform, pissing in a spotlight." "The nerve of some people! Probably some uncouth Franklinville cop. It's within their perimeter of patrol."

Prohaska said nothing as he went up the stairs to the bathroom. His shoes made a "squishing" sound with every step. "Anything wrong with Prohaska?" Salterella asked. I lit up one of the cigars Prohaska had thrown on the desk. "Naw, Sarge, just a case of nervous kidneys."

The cemetery continued to have visitors from our department, although Prohaska was cured of his uncouth habit, another nocturnal spectre haunted the cemetery. His name was Philo Elders.

CHAPTER 25

FILTHY PHILO

Words fail to describe Philo Elders. Where Webster's fails, Psychopathia Sexualis by Kraft-ebbing might do. Although Kraft-Ebbing is a textbook used by psychologists in dealing with case histories of sexual deviates, Philo would have fallen more toward the latter than the former. He in short was definitely an "off the wall" character.

The first time we rode patrol together was back around the Summer of 1977. I heard strange tales of Philo, but never put much stock in them. After all, he was a cop, an officer of the peace and preserver of the law. Philo and I were working the "dog watch" late Saturday evening. As the patrol car passed the Orthodox Cemetery on our Main St., Elders pulled the car onto the roadway that led through the graveyard. We occasionally patrol the area to deter vandalism and sex, even though it is across the Boro line. Philo rolled the car to a stop at the end of the darkened road and cut the engine and lights. "Here's where I initiate all the special officers coming onto the force." Elders announced. His right hand slid across the seat toward me. Before he had a chance to touch me, I brought the heavy lead-cored nightstick gently on his knuckles. "Have you thought of what the rest of your life is going to be like with only a left hand?" I asked in a menacing voice. Philo laughed as he pulled his hand back. "Just kidding, just wanted to get your reaction." I knew he was, but I wasn't. I had been warned of his odd sense of humor by the others. Elders just loved to rattle people with the unexpected. The cemetery sequence was just another way of doing that.

Another way of Philo's jocular metods of "busting chops" was to take a rookie special on his patented "car shakedowns". Taking the old decommissioned patrol car which sat behind headquarters with balding tires and marked "for emergency use only", Philo would take the rattling hulk to the nearest interstate. Once on that four lane expressway, Elders would put on the overhead lights and push the accelerator through the floor, going well over 100 mph, with the front end of the patrol car about to detach itself from the rest of the frame, Elders would holler across to his fear-stricken passenger, "No problem! Just burning out some carbon deposits in the engine>' I speak from experience on the point because I had the misfortune to be on one of his thrill rides. After my initial introduction to high speed auto racing, I cautioned Officer Elders, despite the obvious wet spot between my uniformed pant legs, I would personally bring him up on charges if he did that again….and I lived through it.

Despite our opposite polarities, Philo and I got along rather well. He was outspoken, ribald, sacrilegious, profane and fat, just the opposite of me. I guess that's why we became friends. At least there was no pretense about Philo. "What you see is what you get" as he was fond of saying.

On another evening, Philo came to me and informed me that he was going to work a new special police officer that evening in the patrol car. His name, according to Elders, was Ronnie Espo. "For Christ's sake, please. No screwing around. Straight police work, ok?" I beseeched Elders. "We want to make an impression on him that's positive. He's young and impressionable." Philo just smiled his maniacal little grin. As Espo reported for duty, I pulled him aside before Philo came in and attempted to fill him in on his riding partner. I especially emphasized his cemetery routine. "To be warned is to be fore armed". I wasn't that far from the truth as it turned out. A little after midnight, Philo drove to the cemetery with the rookie on the pretext of checking it out. I guess the temptation was too much for Philo. It went about as he had planned, stopping the car at the end of the road, hand across the seat, everything except Espo's reaction. Espo took out his service revolver and stuck it in Philo's face. "I'll blow your fuckin head off if you ever try a stunt like that again!" Elders broke out into a cold sweat.

Elders looked into Espo's eyes. They told him they meant business. Elders stammered his explanation of his odd introduction for special officers, but Espo had already heard it from me. He just wanted to give Philo an object lesson in human behavior. It had succeeded, because from that time on Philo's cemetery initiation was dropped from his repertoire. I smiled at Espo's retelling of the episode and wished I had used his method of dealing with Philo's stunt after my "death ride" on the expressway. I wondered how Espo would deal with that when his time came. It would come eventually, knowing Philo.

Philo's lust for life sometimes spilled over onto his official police duties. While on patrol late one evening, Edlers clocked a speeding vehicle on River Road, doing considerably over the speed limit. Philo brought the police cruiser quickly up behind the speeding car and hit his lights and siren. The fleeing car pulled to the shoulder of the road, and Philo jumped from his unit. Elders flashed his light into the driver's face as he approached. One should never take chances when on solitary patrol. Better an annoyed driver than a dead cop. The blue eyes his flashlight shone into were built into an attractive blond female face, mounted on a delectable body. Philo's light drifted down to reveal tanned legs extending from a tight pair of cut down jeans. The breathtaking view of her cleavage made Philo momentarily forget what he had stopped her for. "What's the matter officer?", she said with a slight slur. "DWI" thought Philo. "Alright honey, where's the fire?" That trite phrase Philo uttered was about to be embellished beyond his wildest imagination. "Why, it's between my legs, officer. Do you think you have a hose big enough to put it out?" Philo stood stunned. One of the rare moments of speechlessness in his life. Without further ado, Elders leaned into the open car window. He reached his hand into the interior, slipping his hand into her tube top, as he crushed his mouth onto her yielding lips. Releasing his hold on her, Elders opened the car door and pushed her across the seat. Holding in the button on the door that turns on the courtesy lights, he quickly closed the door. On that deserted stretch of highway in the early morning hours, Philo consummated his passion in a police version of Lady Chatterley's game keeper! Elders "did his duty" and enforced the limits of the law to his fullest measure.

The myriad of questions that filled my mind upon his retelling of the incident was answered with, "Where there is a will, there's a way!" As Elders left to resume his patrol, I inquired if he had gotten any information as to whom she was, Philo replied, "Sure, I have all the information I need in my summons book." I looked him in the eye. "Do you mean to tell me..." I began to say. Philo cut me off in mid-sentence. "You're damn right. I gave her a speeding ticket!" "I hope you catch some social disease!" I yelled at his back, as he went out the back door, giggling.

CHAPTER 26

THE GRASS IS ALWAYS GREENER

The newspaper headline leaped out in large print, "DRUG FACTORY DISCOVERED NEXT TO POLICE HEADQUARTERS." The accompanying photo of the Southbrook Police Headquarters and the adjacent building must have been responsible for a lot of spilled coffee that morning. "Why not?" I reasoned. "At least they got good police protection. I'm surprised they didn't think of putting the drug factory in the basement of our Boro Hall, underneath the Chief's Office, for added security!" The "speed and pot" shop had been in operation almost a year right next door to us. The sign over the rented garage annex read, "SPEEDY SERVICE" ...." Speedy?" I thought. Hell, with the amount of money they uncovered, that place could have used the name FEDERAL EXPRESS COURIER SERVICE (when you absolutely have to get high overnight!)

Admittedly, the cover of an auto body shop was a good one. The nightly comings and goings would not seem out of place. And, what better locale than right next to the police. One evening I heard the outside burglar alarm going off next door. I dutifully radioed the patrol car to respond to check out the premises. The police car was met by one of the owners, who explained that he had accidentally tripped the alarm upon closing shop. Probably sampled some of his product.

Somehow, maybe through their network of informants, the County Prosecutor's Office caught wind of the operation. Agents from the Prosecutor's Drug Division came to our department to set up surveillance in the only place that afforded a clear view, the bathroom of police headquarters. The County made one point emphatically clear, under no circumstances was Chief Wildman to be made aware of the surveillance, equipment or the overall investigation. He was to be kept in the dark. No problem that I could foresee. The Chief was always in the dark about activities in headquarters. The equipment was put in our upstairs bathroom and had to be taken out every morning before Chief arrived and installed every evening after he left. The cameras and sound equipment fit into a large suitcase, making it portable. The second-floor stairwell leading to the bathroom was chained off to the public in the evening with a sign which read: "No Admittance to the Public". The precaution was taken so that no unsuspecting person would stumble into the odd assortment of men gathered in our bathroom in the evening. It sometimes resembled a Gay Convention in a closet.

As was bound to happen, a snafu developed one evening, in the person of the Chief. While one of the detectives was monitoring the BBB (bathroom binocular battalion), our leader made a rare evening appearance. Upon seeing his arrival, I sent Hendershot over to alert upstairs while I stalled the Chief. Wildman was in civilian clothes when he entered the back door. "Just came to use the bathroom, Jay", were the first words out of his mouth. My heart sank. I intercepted him at the door leading out to the hallway. "Uh…. Chief, you can't use the bathroom." I was desperately seeking an answer to the question that was inevitably going to follow. "What the hell do you mean? I've got to take a wicked piss!" He was annoyed. "Well, there's a problem in the bathroom." I was beginning to feel like Maxwell Smart. "Would you believe there's a spy in the bathroom?"

Before the Chief could respond, a man with a large suitcase calmly descended the stairs and strode by the Chief and myself at the doorway. Without saying a word to either of us, he opened the front door and was gone. "Who was that", Wildman said. "The Exterminator", I lied. "The exterminator?" the Chief replied. "Yeah. That's the problem. We have roaches in the bathroom. The Boro sent over that man to spray the bathroom." The Chief looked puzzled. "He certainly works odd hours". I looked at the clock on the wall. It was 11 p.m. "Yes, well...the roaches only come out at night, I responded. (Good answer, I thought to myself). The Chief appeared to have taken the "roach-bait". I continued, "I think we got the roaches from the garage next door. They were having a problem with roaches." The roaches in the neighboring garage weren't the kind that scurry around in dark corners, but rather the smoking variety. So, while my story wasn't a total fabrication, it was a gross distortion of the truth. The Chief asked if it was okay to use the bathroom now. "Oh sure, the spray is odorless and colorless", I said with great relief.

The Chief did his duty and came downstairs. As he approached the rear door of headquarters, Wildman turned to me and said "I didn't see any roaches while I was up there. Guess that spray works fast!" The Chief closed the door behind him as he departed, a slightly quizzical expression on his face.

Detective Hendershot, who had been hiding in the office across the hall, emerged from his exile. "Great bullshit job, Jay", he exclaimed, slapping me on the shoulder. "Good enough to be the next Chief?" I inquired. "Better". The old "exterminator-in-the-toilet" spy trick works every time.

CHAPTER 27

THE CUE STICK MURDER

Death came suddenly to the pool hustler, as it sometimes does. A friendly game between two strangers at the bar had developed ugly overtones. Verbal abuse rapidly escalated into a physical confrontation and a cue stick became an instrument of death. What set the spark was muddled in the events that followed; a hurled bar stool, retaliated by a broken cue stick. The stool missed its mark, the jagged stick did not. The shard pierced the midsection of one of the adversaries with such force, it came out through his back! He was pronounced DOA at the Emergency Room. That's when we entered the scene. The murderer was a resident of Southbrook.

The Detectives from the Brunswyck Prosecutor's Office came to our headquarters about 3 a.m., as I was getting off my shift. The two men were accompanied by a third officer from our own County Prosecutor's Office. "We have a warrant for one of your residents". One of the officers stepped forward and produced the paperwork. "The charge is homicide." The look on my face produced a smile from one of the investigators. "Guess you don't get too many murders in a town this size", he ventured. My mind drifted back to 1976, the year I saw my first murder.

Detective Hendershot had classified that one as a murder-suicide. An elderly gentleman had taken a shotgun and discharged one of the two barrels into his terminally ill, bedridden, wife. The blast terminated her years of anguish with brain cancer that had reduced their lives to abject poverty. Surrounded by the squalor of their one room apartment, he sat down next to her bed, covered her corpse gently and stuck the loaded remaining barrel into his mouth and pulled the trigger. We found his body, upright in the chair.

The top of his head, from his eyebrows up, had disappeared, rather disbursed…into a grisly pattern of blood and bone on the far wall. A "Portrait of Death" as painted by the Grim Reaper.

I snapped back into the reality of the moment, and the pool cue murder. "I'll phone for our detective and we will make arrangements", I heard myself speak. Detectives Chin and Hendershot arrived at headquarters within a half hour and exchanged brief cordialities before getting down to business. "Jay", officer Hendershot addressed me. "Arrange for Franklinville to monitor our phone here at the station, you come with me in an unmarked unit." I thought to myself…so much for going home. The detective proceeded to outline his plan of action. Franklinville and Eastbrook would provide backup units to aid us in flushing our quarry. It was now 4 a.m. and I was wide awake, my adrenals pumping high octane into my system. The residence of our suspect on River Road was already staked out by a team. A license plate number had provided the necessary information and the car used in the suspect's flight was sitting in the driveway. All we had to do was go in and get him.

Police units stealthily approached the darkened house. The other units from nearby communities were on post, blocking off the streets near the home. Hendershot covered the back door of the two- story frame house, as two officers approached the front door. The muffled sounds of the walkie talkies broke the still night air. I gripped the stock of my Browning .12 gauge as if to reassure myself. One of the officers tried the doorknob but the door was locked. He then took a few steps back and kicked in the flimsy lock. Both officers flattened themselves against the sides of the doorway as they cast the beams of their flashlights into the black interior. Cautiously, the entered the room. The suspect, in an alcoholic stupor, lay passed out on the couch. With much difficulty, the woke the resident and, ascertaining he was the object of their search, read him his rights and handcuffed him.

I looked at his face as they led him away. It was a look of despair. Clothes in disarray, hair mussed, slumped shoulders, all the characteristics of a defeated man. He was shaking softly as they placed him in the back of the patrol car.

He had fought his own battle with the demon that dwells in all of us. The demon that makes us all potential killers if the right buttons are pushed. Most people win their individual battles, he was part of that small percentage that didn't. Back at headquarters, when asked why he had stuck that jagged cue through the deceased, he said softly, "Because he made a wisecrack." I guess the booze made killing a little easier. That part of us submerged deep in the ID of our psyches burst forth in the white heat of anger and he committed the ultimate transgression: murder.

CHAPTER 28

BLOW OUT

Part of the late-night duties of a police officer is breaking up couples, heterosexual and … whomever; that is, disturbing their "make out" sessions. The biological urges of the libido sometimes seize people in the strangest of places. We've discovered couples making love after dark in the local cemetery under a full moon. Since they were of the same sex, we nicknamed them the "queer wolves". Another time, we caught a male and female in the bathroom of the Municipal Court. Both were defendants in a case and chosen to use our unisex facility at the same time. Lord only knows what transpired that set them aflame with passion at such an inopportune time, but the judge hit them with a Contempt of Court citation. It cost them $50 for forgetting to lock the door. During another instance, a couple was found on the baseball field "pitching" woo. (Pardon the obvious pun). The sergeant called them out at Homeplate for trying an inside the park homer. Most of the activity confined itself to the "parking passion pit" of the Animal House. On any given Spring night there was more action there than at the drive-in.

On one such night, about 3 a.m., Hendershot came flying through the rear door of headquarters. He had spotted a couple going "hot and heavy" inside a van in the passion pit. He had me call in the road patrol to the station. The three of us quietly approached the van in an unmarked car. The van was bouncing back and forth as if caught in a windstorm. It was, I guess, of sorts. Hendershot muttered with a crooked grin, "Nobody has fun when I'm on duty". For Patrolman Elders, arriving in car 27, this kind of activity was "right up his alley." After all, it was a slow shift, nothing much happening, so anything to break up the monotony. We all slipped up on the side of the van. Hendershot to the driver's window, Elders to the front windshield and I moved to the passenger's side window. We slowly rose to peer in the windows. Although we were doing what was technically in the line of duty, it bordered on voyeurism. In retrospect, Hell, it was voyeurism! The male occupant had his pants down and was astride the female. "Christ!" Elders whispered, "he's getting a hummer!" The ecstatic moans that permeated the van's interior made the partners oblivious to their surroundings. "Now!" Henderson yelled. In ballet-like unison, we sprang the beams of our powerful flashlights into the windows. "Police officers!" Hendershot shouted as he pounded on the window. The male jumped up and attempted to zip up his fly. The action was mechanical. The results were painful. His organ got caught in the zipper and he hollered in agony as he fell between the front seats. The girl calmly rearranged herself and rolled down the sweaty windows. I looked at Elders face. The windows weren't the only thing sweating. "Sorry, but you're in violation of Boro ordinance by committing such acts in public", Hendershot sternly spoke. "Please move the vehicle immediately or I'll have to arrest you both."

The threat of public disclosure prompted the couple to comply. The male occupant's muffled anguish was evident as the girl started the engine. "You may want to stop off at the ER", Elders volunteered, "*somebody else* should look at that!" The girl smiled and told Elders to go fuck himself, as she slammed the van into gear and took off. As the vehicle hit the curb at the parking lot exit, the "boyfriend" wailed at an even higher pitch. Another crime foiled by the relentless pursuit of justice. The day crew were puzzled when the found a hand-written over the police desk next morning. In stenciled Gothic, the cardboard sign revealed the new motto of the midnight shift: "WE PEEP WHILE OTHERS SLEEP".

CHAPTER 29

THE BETTER PART OF VALOR

As Deputy Director of Administration for the "Blue Stripes", I have occasion to ride patrol in the marked units of the Boro. It's an experience every citizen should have at least once to better appreciate what the average policeman copes with on the "mean" streets. The night of July 28, 1978 descended, hot and sultry. Car 27 was manned by me and Detective Hendershot, who was filling a tour of duty for a sick officer. Well into an otherwise uneventful shift, we received a backup call to assist in a "domestic" going down in neighboring Eastbrook. Hendershot hit the lights and sirens he slammed down on the pedal. We briefly exchanged knowing glances. Every officer *hates* to roll on "domestic" fights. They are the most potentially explosive calls an officer makes. An officer knows what to expect in a robbery-in-progress call, but "domestics" as a rule, are most dangerous because often the responding officers become the focal point of the aggression. We both hoped the call would be an exception to the rule.

The sirens and lights were cut well before we turned into the street that was lined with manicured lawns and neat middle-class homes. The pulsating red strobe lights of the Eastbrook patrol car guided us to the house we sought. I glanced at my watch as I called out at location. It is 2 a.m. "Why don't people start fighting at respectable times", I thought to myself as I exited the car. We met the Eastbrook patrolman in front of the house. He was a large Irishman with a stomach protruding well over his gun belt. I noted he was a Special police officer with no partner. Hence, most likely, the need for the back up from our town. "I'm the only cop on tonight. The other cars are out of service, and my partner called in sick", he spoke as we climbed the steps. We were met at the door by a distraught female, her left cheek red swollen. She pointed to the top of the steps. "The bastard's locked himself in the bathroom on the second floor", she spat out her words with venom. With Eastbrook officer staying at the foot of the steps with the woman, Hendershot and I slowly ascended the steps to the second floor. A light shone under the bathroom door in the otherwise dark hallway. I positioned myself with a clear view of the door as Hendershot switched on the hall light and rapped firmly on the door. "Police officers. Come out now! We want to talk to you!" He door opened slowly as Hendershot took a couple of quick steps backward. The moment was filled with uncertainty and anxiety. Would he come out fighting or docile? In retrospect, I'm glad it was the latter. The offending husband emerged from the bathroom slowly. Actually, "unfolded" out of the bathroom would be more accurate. I looked on in awe as he bent his head to clear the six-foot nine-inch doorframe. "Damn!" I uttered under my breath, the guy must be 6' 10" and at least 275 pounds.

As Hendershot ushered the man into an adjacent bedroom, I pulled at his arm. "Discretion is the better part of valor", I whispered in his ear. I knew he felt the same way. It would not have been possible to "take" the husband if he got violent. The "behemoth's" weight was more than ours put together, and I judged him to be in excellent physical health. Besides, I rationalized, why get injured, or even maimed, on a call in another town where they couldn't even backup their own officers. Besides that, the word maimed had such a finality to it. I visualized the headlines: "TWO POLICEMEN MAIMED ON A MISSION OF MERCY". That is the type of alliterative headline you might read in the National Enquirer next to "MY MOTHER HAD AN AFFAIR WITH BIGFOOT". Diplomacy became the "watchword" as we tried to diffuse the situation. I went downstairs and asked the wife if she had any place she could stay for the evening, as she had indicated earlier, she did not want to sign a complaint. She nodded affirmatively. If she wanted to change her mind about the complaint she could do so in the morning. I then went upstairs and aided Hendershot with the more pressing matter of the husband.

I introduced Hendershot and myself to him, which seemed to put him a bit off guard. When the husband started a dialogue on why the situation got out of hand, I felt we were on the right track. "My wife and I are going to separate. I sort of lost my head". In questioning him further, we ascertained that he was a computer systems analyst with an excellent job in a well-known company. Obviously intelligent, I ventured to say that if he had to be arrested, it would likely put his job in jeopardy. I had made my point.

By this time, the wife had left with a relative and the problem seemed to be resolved for the moment. The man left alone as the three of us went into the house.

A week later, I saw the same officer in Eastbrook. I inquired about of "venture" that night and if the situation has been resolved. He laughed, "I didn't work the next night, but all hell broke loose in that house! He threw two cops down the steps and sent them to the hospital." 'Were they maimed?' (I felt an impulse to ask). Since it happened on my day off and involved the Eastbrook police, the information had not yet reached me. I thought as I left the officer, "There but for the grace of God, go I." and Hendershot too for that matter. The difference sometimes between being maimed and being healthy, is discretion....and a little luck!

CHAPTER 30

THE 65% SOLUTION

Dimo was the new cop, "green" and eager as they usually are. His first week on the job, and already he had gone through two complete traffic ticket books. Dimo "slapped paper" on anything that moved in the Boro, including a fellow officer of the Special Police. It goes without saying, he heard about that at headquarters. "You gave Kaminski a ticket for parking to close to an intersection?" I asked. He could tell I was somewhat offended. To compound the breach of etiquette, the car he ticketed was parked in front of Millstone's house. John Dimo knew the distinctive van Kaminski drove, but he wrote it up anyhow. "John, you can't start a precedent like this", I said. "Otherwise, we'll have cops out for revenge, writing up other cops. Next time, knock on the door and have the vehicle moved."

All rookies are the same. They try to set the world on fire, until they realize their matches are in limited supply. Eventually, the doldrums of police work begin to set in, the monotonous daily routine, the bleary-eyed rotating shifts, the mind-numbing double shifts, all of which take their toll. Then the rookie settles into the background of conformity and obscurity, especially with Chief Wildman at the helm. Actually, in our department, it was a blessing to be obscure, for no one wanted to be held long in the Chief's thoughts.

Dimo and I became obscure to Wildman. I, because I worked the late shifts, and Dimo because of his newness to the force. You could gauge your obscurity index by the amount of times the Chief mispronounced your name. When he began to get your name correct, you were on his mind, and that meant trouble. Dimo was still "Prina", "Leno", "Promo". He was still safe.

One evening I chose to ride home with John Dimo. It was an unfortunate choce. We were parked in the lot of an all 24-hr convenience store, monitoring the local scumbags, when we were greeted by a dispatcher for the "County Mounties", who was doing some last- minute shopping. K As she bade farewell and crossed the lot, she was accosted by a drunk. This guy made the zombies of "Thriller" look inviting. Her yell alerted us, and we both jumped from the patrol car. Chivalry was NOT dead for Dimo. A genuine damsel in distress. Up to this time, the drunk was rather harmless and hadn't really done more than frighten her. John asked the inebriated young man to produce ID. He ignored John's request and began to pass into the store. Each time he took a step, Dimo stepped in front of him and asked again for ID. His request again was met with an escalating profusion of obscenities. Dimo directed that I call for a backup unit. I smelled a brawl. I could also smell drunk, phew! Marinated in Muscatel. Dimo was going to take him.

Up to now, John Dimo had controlled himself admirably. The drunk said he lived nearby, but John insisted on seeing some ID. Redness was creeping up John's neck, visible even under the fluorescent lights. I requested a backup at our location. Hendershot and Prohaska were at headquarters for the change of shifts. Having made the call, I slipped up behind the agitated drunk and made ready to back Dimo's move. I didn't have long to wait.

"Alright, that's it. You are under arrest!" Dimo shouted. He commenced to grab the man by the arm while at the same time reaching to the rear of his gunbelt for his handcuffs. Although Dimo was 6'2" and had an athletic build, he soon has his hands full of the angry drunk. A brief struggle ensued and both men tumbled to the ground. Dimo's badge was ripped from his uniform. I took out my nightstick and pinned one of his arms with my knee. We could not, despite all efforts, cuff our squirming madman. "God dammit!" Dimo swore, "I'll handle him. See what the hell has happened to our backup!"

I reluctantly ran back to the patrol car and growled into the mike, "699, WHERE THE HELL IS OUR BACKUP – OFFICERS NEED ASSISTANCE!" I dropped the received and ran back to Dimo, who by this time had cuffed on of the suspect's hands. My arrival at Dimo's side coincided with the arrival of our backup. Hendershot and Prohaska tumbled out of the car and ran toward us. A handful of "bros" had gathered to witness yet another example of "Police brutality". "Hey, man", shouted one in the crowd, "that dude ain't done nuthin'…. let him be". We were too busy to pay heed to the multitude. The four officers picked up the drunk and carried him to the patrol car. He was deposited across the hood while attempts were made to cuff his other hand and put on leg shackles. Our attempts proved futile and the violence of the mob escalated to a higher level. "Screw this", I said, and ran to the opposite side of the hood, nearest his bobbing head. The crowd was getting larger, and obviously more hostile. "Hey, pigs….sommatta? Ain't got enough muscle?" They jeered at our attempt at humane treatment. They took it as a sign of weakness, which made them progressively bolder. We had to end this struggle soon, or our friend might receive reinforcements. I reached over the hood; the end of my nightstick grasped in my hands. I hooked the center of the stick underneath the suspect's jaw and pulled back. The choking action temporarily cut off his oxygen supply, as it snapped his head down against the hood. As his air supply was reduced, so was his will to fight. He was quickly subdued, cuffed, and thrown into the rear of the car. Our attention was now diverted to the crowd, from which a woman came forward. "Jesse! That's my Jesse you got!" she shouted. Officer Hendershot stopped her just short of the backup car. She identified herself as the older sister. We advised her she could pick up Jesse at headquarters as soon as bail was set. We really had no intention of letting him go of course. Jesse was going to jail. Maybe just for the weekend, but he was going. Jesse was a cop-fighter, and this is the unwritten mandate…Fight a cop, go to jail, do not pass GO, pay $200.

The next evening, Hendershot and I were riding together in an unmarked vehicle. We passed Dimo in an alley, with car 27. He was on radar, sitting with his car lights, his spider web of tentacles ready to ensnare an unwary errant driver. We were three hours into the midnight shift, when the detective decided (this was rapid-fire for him!), "Let's bust Dimo's tomatoes", obviously referring to his genitalia, not his backyard garden.

I inquired tentatively into the nature of this "fun". "I'll show you," Hendershot replied with that devilish smile. He unfolded his plot. Dimo was not familiar with this unmarked car. It was a dark night, no moon. Hendershot maneuvered out of radar range of Dimo's patrol car. Suddenly, Hendershot floored the gas of this powerful V8, the acceleration slamming me back into the seat. The speedometer rose, 60-70-80 mph. I swore softly to myself and made remission for my past sins, as the speedometer hit 90. Oh, and don't forget the sin of stupidity for ever getting into the same car with Hendershot or Elders.

Dimo must have wet his pants as the car hurled into the radar's range. I could hear the audible doppler alarm screaming in my mind. "Car 27 to headquarters. I just had somebody blow by my position at nearly 100 mph, heading West on Main Street!".

"Hmmm", muttered Hendershot, "our speedometer must be off by a little." Fantastic! I thought. We are about to meet our Maker and he's worried about an uncalibrated speedometer! When Dimo asked as to the whereabouts of Car 28, Hendershot gave him a fictitious location. Dimo was having trouble bringing Car 27 back to life to give pursuit, which was evidenced by the profanities I heard him mutter into the dying car radio. Oh, and did I mention the dead car battery? His "big score" disappeared down Main Street.

Hendershot suppressed his glee as he radioed to the stranded rookie, "We'll get him, John. No worries!" As Dimo fumed, Hendershot parked his car in a secluded alleyway. We put our feet on up the dash and commenced to give a blow-by-blow description of our "pursuit".

After an appropriate length of time, Hendershot terminated the chase by losing the suspect's vehicle before he got close enough to get the plate number. We called in to the desk for a "30" at headquarters.

We parked the car behind headquarters and entered the back door just as Dimo came in from his disabled unit and entered the front door. It was change of shift time and fellow officers were coming on. "Call the hook", the frustrated patrolman requested, which meant call the tow truck. Dimo looked at our faces and noticed small grins on both, as we feigned being busy with paperwork. "Something funny?" he said. The grins got wider. Hendershot said something to the effect that it was a shame that Dimo missed that speeder. Dimo's scowl was gradually replaced by a small smile as Hendershot continued his commiserations. Dimo pressed his inquiry further, "Do you guys know something I don't?" That brought forth an eruption of laughter from both of us.

Dimo's suspicions were fully aroused now, but he could not get us to say any more on the subject. As Dimo and I left through the back door, he caught sight of the unmarked car, the color matched that of the speeder. Our actions plus a look at the car finally "hit home". "You know, I'm 65% sure that I'm the butt of some wise-ass joke and that you guys are at the bottom of it!"

The roar of laughter that followed from the figure at the door was further confirmation of his suspicions. From that day forward, Dimo earned the nickname "65% Dimo".

CHAPTER 31

CHARLIE "CHIN" AND THE CASE OF THE ROTTEN RUBBER

It isn't often that tires become an object of a department investigation, but these tires were a bit out of the ordinary. They were mounted on a police car. They almost cost the life of a police officer engaged in a high-speed pursuit. Cameron was chasing a "4-50" (drunk driver) on a nearby Interstate, when a sudden vibration in the front end of the patrol car sent the vehicle out of control. The car spun onto the grassy divider strip that separated the opposing lanes of traffic.

After the aborted chase, LoSanta and I were at headquarters when Cameron made his entrance. "I can't figure it out", he said. "I could have sworn the tire blew, the way the car behaved." When Cameron had checked the car on the divider, the tires were apparently intact. The tires were new, having been put on the previous day. The three of us went out back to examine the car. As I bent down to look at the suspect rubber more closely, I noticed a distorted tread and fine cracks in the sides of both tires. "Are you sure these tires are brand new?" I inquired. The tires did not have the look of newness about them. Upon closer inspection I could see the letters "N/A" burned into the inside of each tire. I copied the codes that appeared on each wheel. I went inside to put in a phone call to a friend who is in the tire business. (He's also into whips and chains, but that's another story). I got him on the phone and asked about the N/A on the tires. He confirmed my suspicions. The letters were branded into the tires as a warning. They mean overaged, not for road use.

The one big question remained in our minds; i.e., how did the detective's tires get on our patrol car? LoSanta dug up the bill for payment in the amount of $70, made out to Bill's Gas

Station for two polyglass belted radials. I logged a note into the desk book that the vehicle was not to be used until the situation was fixed. I then wrote a formal request for an investigation into the matter. Neither LoSanta nor Cameron would sign the request. "The Chief approved of the purchase, and Detective Chin acted on that approval, right?" LoSanta reasoned in his methodical style. "That means that the investigation will have to go right to the Commissioner. The politicians upstairs will be gone in two years, and we will have to live with the Chief and Chin for the rest of our time in the department!" LoSanta liked the politicos only slightly more than a case of genital herpes. He trusted them even less. It was understandable. Why should he and Cameron jeopardize their careers and pin their hopes on the politicians to uncover what could be a nasty expose. "You sign it, Jay", LoSanta urged. Without their testimony, I didn't stand a chance of seeing justice prevail. I pondered the request for a while, then ripped it up and threw it in the trash can. "You're learning", LoSanta smirked. I left headquarters and slammed the door behind me. "Yeah, I'm learning, and it hurts", I mumbled to no one in particular.

The next evening, as I came on duty, I spotted the patrol car parked against the gray rail fence to the right of the entrance. I noticed also that it was sporting two new front tires. Walking through the back door, LoSanta, anticipating my question, spoke. "Looks like your log entry got the job done, Jay." "Pizza tonight!" I said. "Yeah, and I'll buy", was the reply from LoSanta. I managed a weak smile. LoSanta was educating me almost day by day. I was tempted to overlook an occasional aberration such as the time he stole a car.

CHAPTER 32

G.T.A.

Grand Theft Auto is ordinarily NOT a crime that is committed by a police officer. The provocation in this case, however, was understandable…the Animal House.

An employee of this establishment made it a habit to leave his running car, unattended, at the employees' door at the rear of the building. As a result, more than once the vehicle was "borrowed" by those inhabiting the joint. "Jungle Jim", who was usually tighter than a $5 pair of shoes, could not seem to bring himself to leave at the appointed closing time. Time and time again, Jim would come crashing into headquarters, screaming his car had been stolen and wanting to file a complaint. Usually, it would appear, parked somewhere else in the lot, or as happened once, in a nearby canal spirited away by mutual admirers with similarly malevolent behavioral problems. His auto situation accounted for 25% of the stolen car reports our department handled that year.

LoSanta and Cameron were on patrol, while I administered the last rites to a dying typewriter at headquarters. It was an unusually warm night in October, and through the open window I heard a commotion sweeping up our front steps. Somebody was shouting, although I could not make out the words, the tone spelled trouble. The door swung open, and in stumbled "Jungle Jim". Actually "fell through" would be a better description, for, as usual, he was "feeling no pain". Good thing, too, as I noticed his nose was gone, or splattered over the center of his face. He pushed himself upright against the wall, his face and shirt soaked in blood. "Somebody stole my car!" he anguished. "I want to file a complaint!" Better make that two complaints", I countered, "somebody stole your nose too!" Poor Jim, he had gone back into the bar and accused a bartender of theft (he had done it

129

once before, according to my recollection). The accused took affront to the charge and remodeled Joe's face with a beer bottle.

I summoned the patrol car to headquarters. While awaiting its arrival, a second person came into headquarters bearing an icepack, which he promptly applied to where Jim's nose had been. "I'm sorry, Jim. But you oughtn't go around accusing people of stealing your stuff", his voice truly remorseful. Jim just dripped and sobbed a little.

LoSanta and Cameron came through the back door. I gave them a rundown on what has transpired. LaSanta asked Jim if he still wished to sign a complaint. Jim was wavering. The bartender volunteered to take Jim to the hospital for repairs, all of us agreeing it was an excellent idea. Jim and his former advisory took off together, complaints would be filled out tomorrow if Jim wished.

I told LoSanta I was going to call county dispatch and put out an alert for the missing car. Cameron stopped me. "We know where the car is. LoSanta and I will go and get it." He stated this rather matter-of-factly. "How do you know where the car is?" I questioned him. "Because, I took it!" LoSanta replied.

I fell back against my chair, looking at the two officers. "You stole Jungle Jim's car?" I repeated in an incredulous tone. LoSanta explained, "I'm sick and tired of him stumbling in here yelling that his damn car's been stolen. He leaves the son-of-a-bitch running in the parking lot for hour. He's just asking for trouble, so I decided to teach him a lesson."

I heard myself bark, "So, you, an officer of the law, decide to steal his car?" "Not steal, just borrow and move to a new location", was his defense. "Great!" I said. "We can down grade the charges to taking a vehicle without the owner's permission", my voice dripped with sarcasm. I had no intention of letting this matter go any further, nor was it my intent to get LoSanta into trouble. Except for Jim's nose, it was a prank with some unexpected repercussions. No problem.

"Look, LoSanta. Just make sure that car is parked where he left it, so when he gets back from "Five Oh" he finds it in the place where it was last seen." I cautioned the officers. Cameron shot back, "Shit, in his condition, he couldn't find a nymphomaniac in a whorehouse!" I opened my mouth to say something, "I know, I know…" he was out the door before I could form a sentence. I was a one-legged man in an ass-kicking contest. I couldn't do anything either way, nor would I. Best let things develop in their own way. I wasn't going to jeopardize the careers of two fine officers over a lush who didn't have sense enough to unzip his pants to piss!

I made the brief log entries. "2:30 a.m., Car Reported Missing". "3:30 a.m., Car Found."

Accompanied by the appropriate information. I sat back and thought for a bit. It was all about "conditioned response". Car misplaced. Jim comes to headquarters to complain. Car found. How many times this scenario repeated itself. It was all conditioned response. Just like Pavlov's dog. Maybe this time the cycle will be broken. But I mused with an internal grin, Pavlov's dog didn't get his nose broke……

CHAPTER 33

NOBODY CRIES FOR JOEY BINGO

Memories. The bitter residue of years of law enforcement. Shootings, stabbings, rapes, mayhem, murder. You name the motives.... revenge, domestic squabbles, sex, whatever.... the results were always the same, a corpse. Sometimes, just pieces of a corpse.

Even before I became a cop, murder was unfamiliar to me. Our neighbor across the street beheaded her elderly mother whom she had attended, having to give up her vital years, giving up the sweet wine of youth. The wine turned to vinegar as the daughter grew more and more bitter. The constant demands of her mother over those twenty years cast her into the tortured limbo of the murderer. She put her severed mother's head into a hat box and took it to the State Capitol Building, driving up the marble steps and flinging it in front of the great bronze doors.

We often discover the "who" and the "how" of a thing, but not always the "why". Joey Bingo was a cop. He killed a lot of people in the line of duty. Each was "justifiable". Some say he practiced his own version of pre-trial intervention. It was tough for the dead to testify against him.

It was 1958, the docile decade was coming to an end when my doorbell rang. I opened the door of my parent's home and saw before me the cherubic face of Joey Bingo. He was in uniform, fresh out of police academy. "Here's your gun permit", he said. It was good to see a neighborhood kid uniform. A lot of the kids hadn't gone down that path and a few were in jail. I'd had my share of scrapes with the law, but in a tough neighborhood, that was SOP. Some of the tough ones even became cops. Charlie "Knuckles", one of the best hub-cap snatchers in the area is now Chief of Detectives in a nearby city. I wonder if he still has the caps from my '58 Edsel?

Joey Bingo grew up around the corner from me. A bony kid with a ready smile, he was proud of his uniform. A year later, as I remember it, he was involved in his first shooting. I forget the circumstances, but it was ruled a "clean" shooting, which caused a local uproar in the minority community. Joey quietly left the "our town's" police department for the greener pastures of the big city police in Brunswyck. With him went his reputation for having a "Wyatt Earp" syndrome; you know, shoot first and then advise the suspect of his rights.

The next two shootings occurred over a rather brief period. The first resulted in the death of two Hispanics. The way the story went, the two were stopped for a motor vehicle violation on the main drag of Brunswyck. The male and female occupants of the banged-up Chevy were lit up in the summer darkness by the patrol cars' headlights. A single officer approached the vehicle, Joey Bingo, shotgun in hand, approached from the passenger's side, "Put your hands on the dashboard, where I can see them, both of you!" he commanded. Through the open window, he watched intently as the suspects made movements. According to the officer, the passenger, the male, made a furtive move by dropping his left hand in between the seats. (His left hand was furthest from the officer's vision). Bingo instinctively tensed and yanked open the passenger door, levelling the shogun at the occupants. His tenseness also affected his trigger finger. It discharged as the car door flung open. The body weight of the two victims was instantly increased by the impact of a load of "00" buckshot, the equivalent of being simultaneously struck by nine .38 caliber hollow point bullets. At point blank range, the result was utter devastation.

Coroner's Report: "Massive traumatic injuries to the upper torsos of both victims, caused by a singular discharge from the officer's weapon." That's what the official report said. What Joey did was disintegrate two human torsos from the waist up. Joey stood paralyzed. The gore, a combination of brains, heavy gristle and blood, oozed down the front of his uniform after the blast. A single eyeball, atop the dash, it's vacant stare gazed out at Bingo as he heaved his guts into the gutter.

Amazingly, Joey hung in with the department, despite the public outcry and unanswered questions. Cops cover each other's asses. When there's a question of liability, spelled MONEY, some of the politicians helped shovel the dirt on the question of culpability. Of course, this was 1960, things are different now, aren't they?

Joey was confined to administrative duty for the next year until the storm of protests had subsided. He was then allowed to "serve and protect". One month on the streets and again he dispensed death with his .38 for the fourth time.

Responding to a "robbery in progress" call, Joey was part of the two- man patrol sent to back up the initial response unit. Officer Bingo was sent around to the read of the building to cover the exit, supposedly out of harm's way. As fate would have it, 'twas not to be. Making his way down the alley to the rear, Joey saw something move in the shadows up ahead. He unholstered his "instant justice", cocked the hammer and clicked on his flashlight. The beam caught the figure of a man fleeing toward the fix foot brick wall at the rear of the property. "Halt, Police!" Joey roared. The suspect froze in his tracks, his back to the patrolman. The officer ordered the suspect to turn around very slowly. At five paces, Joey thought he saw something shiny in the hands of the male Hispanic. At four paces, the object was perceived as a switchblade. In three paces, the 16-year old lay dead. A bullet severed his aorta as it tore through his chest.

There were only two witnesses to the incident, and one was now dead. Justification for the shooting was found wanting. This time the dice were loaded against Joey. The dead suspect had a "knife", the cop had a gun, a slight disadvantage on the side of the criminal, even at three feet. Questions. Why would the suspect advance on an armed police officer? Why didn't the officer call for backup? Why did the dead suspect, as the officer claimed, refuse to drop the weapon when ordered to do so?

Too much happened when Joey was around, both past and present. The press had a field day, especially when the subsequent investigation revealed the weapon in the kid's hand was a plastic silver comb that opened like a switchblade!

Joey was fired, and never brought to trial on the shooting. He just faded into obscurity. Twenty- five years later, I still wonder what or how changed that smiling, gangly kid into a walking slaughterhouse. Maybe, if psychological testing was mandatory instead of discretionary, we might have an answer. But we don't, so I will always be curious as to what lit the fuse on the time bomb that lurked in Joey, and in all of us.

CHAPTER 34

OF DREAMS LONG FORGOTTEN

Remember saving Good Humor ice cream wrappers for prizes? Popsicle Pete, Ju-Ju-Bees? Cracker Jack prizes that really were exciting? When Hershey Bars were a nickel? The innocence of the 1950's was long forgotten, except for an occasional thought of Joey Bingo. Every now and then they 'old gang' resurrected itself in my memory.

The Jack Daniels from last night left my mouth feeling like my old wool army socks. I picked up today's paper and glanced at the headline over my morning coffee. "Cop Indicted for Murder of Four-Year Old Son". The headline ripped through my cob-webbed brain. The name of the officer was all too familiar to me. Another of the neighborhood crowd that made a wrong turn on the convoluted road of life. From age eleven to when he'd become a cop, we were friends. Not one of the inner circles of three or four that I considered 'tight', but a street corner buddy. You know, the one who we met every night under the arc-light, but you were never in his home. In Richie's case, his hangout was the bowling alley, "George's Bowling Alley".

We drifted apart after I got married and moved out of the Hungarian section of town. We bumped into each other now and again and talked long and hard about then and now. I looked at the accompanying photo of his puffy face and expressionless eyes and thought back. The dimpled smile, the sparkling blue eyes and that blond hair that fell with a curl over his forehead, were gone. Replacing that was a "zombie" I barely recognized. I slammed my first down on the table with such force, the coffee cup shattered against the saucer beneath. "Son-of-A-Bitch! What happened between 14 and 40?" I asked myself. What should have been, was summed up on the bold type of page one:

"The officer, coming home in a drunken rage over a missing personal item, accused the boy. He administered a beating which culminated in his picking up the child and smashing his head on the concrete floor of the basement."

This beating was not the first, but it certainly was the last. The child died an hour later at the hospital, where he was brought for "falling down a flight of stairs." A medical examination revealed that, if the fractured skull had not killed him, the various damage to his tiny bodily organs from earlier abuse would have.

Alcohol. As a copy, I've seen it used too much as an excuse for violent behavior. The mutilated bodies claimed by drunk drivers, the scarred bodies and faces at police headquarters, the incoherent slobs defecating while taking a breathalyzer test.... yea, I've seen it all. What gets to me is the amount of drunk driving cops that are "cut slack" by their fellow lawmen. A cop who was drunk driving and not caught manning a roadblock the next day, and then passing judgment on some asshole coming home drunk from a Christmas party. Police administrators in the past have shoved departmental drinking under the rug, unable or unwilling to deal with this most persistent of problems. Probably because the job itself is responsible for so much alcohol abuse. Rotating shifts, constant contact with "scumbags" day in and day out, isolation of the officer from the community causing a type of in-bred social relationship with other officers exclusively, even so far as to exclude his own family and children. "My wife doesn't understand", but his fellow officers do. Young rookies, instead of going out on dates, hang around headquarters waiting for something to 'break', to get that high when a felony goes down and the transmitter light flashes with its hypnotic "call to action". Psychologically, or in sociological terms, an officer is easy prey for the snake pit of alcoholism from which few escape unscathed.

Hell, in most states, if you kill with premeditation, you are going to prison for life, or face the death penalty. Use a car to execute somebody and in many states, you can be out in a few years, if that. If you run over someone while under the influence, your lawyer plea bargains "due to diminished capacity" and you literally can get away with murder. Oh yes, you will have your driving privileges suspended also.

I remember the time Richie and I were tugging at a bottle of "Rock & Rye" behind the bowling alley where we once worked. "R & R" was the "in" drink for the youth in those days. We were "pinboys". 12 cents a game and all the wooden splinters under the fingernails you'd ever want. I'll always wonder if it all started then, his spiraling downhill.

The last time I saw Richie was 12 years ago. I lost all contact with him until I picked up the evening paper. He got 30 years to life. He'll be 75 when he's eligible for parole. Until then, he will never touch another drop of booze. No chance for him to fall off the wagon.

CHAPTER 35

COKE EYES

Another bowling alley buddy, "Coke Eyes" got his nickname from the incredible amount of the carbonated soft drink he was able to consume. Some say that is how all his front teeth rotted out. His smile was a visitation from a block-toothed specter of "halitosis". I can picture him leaning against a lava-light Wurlitzer Jukebox whose rainbow fingers of light beckoned the unwary teenager to drop a nickel for your favorite tune. "

"Coke Eyes" favorite number was Frankie Lane's "The Kids Last Fight." At least, I think that was the title. "Come on kid, hit him with a left and a right.....but how were they to know it was the kid's last fight..." Something like that. In those days, they wrote lyrics you can understand, especially when you heard them fifty times a night.

He was big, strong and naturally mean. In some people, meanness is an acquired trait. In Coke Eyes, it came naturally. He was born mean. When the doctor slapped him on the ass for the first breath of life, Coke responded by hitting him in the balls. Everybody cut him slack, even the owner of the lanes, "George the Nose". Even when Coke broke "Duckey's" arm by throwing a pin at him. He would end up paying the Doctor's bill, but the law never interfered with him. Liability? Hell, today, Duckie's parents would have sued the shit out of him, and probably gotten the bowling alley as well.

It came to pass that Coke Eyes received a higher calling in line with his natural aggressive tendencies. He became a cop. Despite his character flaws, he nearly lasted out his probationary year. One of his nastier habits cost him his job. He would stop lone female motorists and ask them, "Do you want to fuck?" I asked him about his carnal inquiries. He said he got his face slapped nine out of ten times…. but it was the tenth one that made it all worthwhile!

At least, so he thought. On traffic duty one evening at a malfunctioning traffic light, Coke spotted a likely subject for his libidinous proposal. He put up his hand and stopped the vehicle. His huge bulk ambled over to the beautiful redhaired occupant. She was reaching for her credentials, thinking she had violated some statute, when he stuck his head through the open car window. Also, the credentials Coke sought could not be found in any glove compartment. He eyed her voluptuous form. "Put that stuff away", he said in a visceral manner. "I'm not looking for that!" The puzzled woman said "Then, why did you stop me?" A toothy smirk curled up the lips of the officer; whereupon, he put forth his proposition, complete with all its Anglo-Saxon crudeness.

Those were probably the last official words he spoke in uniform. The formidable redhead with the fabulous frame was the Police Commissioner's wife!

Duly reporting the incident to her husband, officer "Coke Eyes" was quietly dismissed from the force, after he received a late-night call from an irate Commissioner.

I lost track of Coke Eyes after that. He moved out of the neighborhood and was only seen one time driving through town. Gone, but not forgotten, like so many of my memories, buried beneath the shifting sands of time, only to be one day uncovered by a brainstorm of reflection.

CHAPTER 36

THE WILDMAN GOES 'OVER THE EDGE'

I have a lot in common with a Proctologist. We both work with assholes! The Chief sat in his office, not unlike a feudal king overseeing his serfdom. The morning sunlight streaming in over his back gave an aura of benevolence. More aptly, on of benevolent despotism.

As I strolled into his office, I suppressed the overwhelming urge to genuflect in the presence of such a beatific vision. Endeavoring to plant the seeds of discord into his fertile field of his imagination, I walked up to the window to his back. "You know, Chief," I mused, "Any one of your enemies ("legion" was their name), could get a clean shot at you through this window." A head shot would have ricocheted off his concrete wall, but I wanted to start his work week off with "food for thought".

Wildman dismissed my observation in a cavalier fashion and a nervous laugh. "Hey, if they want to get me...they'll get me anywhere!" The suggestion I implanted, however, was sure to germinate in the rich manure of his mind. What I did not realize was how fast the fruition would be.

Then next day, I had a personal day off. It was not until Wednesday that I returned to headquarters. As I pulled into the parking lot behind his office, I noticed workmen putting the finishing touches on a cover over the Chief's "Achilles Heel", the infamous window mentioned earlier. Chuckling to himself, I surmised that what was thought to be plywood, could at least block any target of opportunity. That would provide a quick solution to our department's promotional logjam.

A closer inspection of the 4 x 6 shield confirmed by deepest desire (that is, other than being on a deserted island with Loni Anderson). The Chief was nearer to commitment than I had previously thought. The "barrier" was not constructed of plywood as initially suspected. It was quarter inch steel!

CHAPTER 37

ALL'S WELL THAT ENDS WELL

Chief yelled, "Cameron! You arrest him!" Cameron stared hard at the Chief for a moment. His face was flushed with a combination of anger and embarrassment. Without answer the Chief, Cameron turned to me and said, "I've got to go out on a call." With that, he wheeled around and went out the back door. The door slammed with such force; the knob flew off. Wildman stood stunned, his mouth agape. This was an obvious act of insubordination. Inwardly, I cheered Cameron's actions. He knew there were no grounds for a legal arrest, other than be a party to a false arrest lawsuit.

I knew my turn was coming. He turned and looked me in the eye, "Jay, YOU arrest him!" "On what grounds, Chief?" The Chief fumbled for a couple of minutes. Then the light went on at the end of his tunnel-dark mind. "He…he…knocked off my hat!" "Chief", I said wearily. "You accidentally knocked off your hat with your hand." I then suggested tactfully, since he was Chief of Police, *he* arrest the man. I rose from the desk and went out the back, leaving Wildman alone with "Chips".

The episode sealed my fate at headquarters as far as Wildman was concerned. When I discovered Wildman was having me followed by Millstone and others in plain clothes to "get something on me", I knew it was time to move on. Millstone was embarrassed when he told me. Not that I had anything to hide, but, Jeez, how much Wildman could one man take? Eleven years was my limit. I served my time in "Hell" as the Marines once put it. I submitted my resignation to the Boro Council.

Wildman's joy was short-lived. I subsequently ran for Mayor the following November, the same year as my resignation, and won by a landslide. The Chief knew I was out

145

to get him, as was evidenced by some campaign rhetoric concerning "mismanagement of the Police Department", etc.

The Chief put in for early retirement in December. He left office January 1. His passage into history was satisfying enough. I did not press any further investigation into department matters.

Justice, after all, had triumphed. After one year in office, I resigned. My primary target had faded into retirement, with the entire force waiting for him to slip off that tightrope he walked....as LoSanta once said, "It may take a little time.... but we *always* get our man."

THE END

www.ingramcontent.com/pod-product-compliance
Lightning Source LLC
Chambersburg PA
CBHW022111280326
41933CB00007B/346

* 9 7 8 0 5 7 8 8 7 5 4 0 8 *